Harcourt Brace School Publishers

TEACHING RESOURCES
Grade 6

Harcourt Brace & Company

Orlando • Atlanta • Austin • Boston • San Francisco • Chicago • Dallas • New York • Toronto • London

http://www.hbschool.com

Printed in the United States of America

ISBN 0-15-311335-9

1 2 3 4 5 6 7 8 9 10 073 2000 99 98

Harcourt Brace School Publishers

Contents

Harcourt Brace School Publishers

Health Handbook for Teachers

Table of Contents

Harcourt Brace School Publishers

A Healthful Classroom

Health Education Today

One hundred years ago most of the illnesses that concerned society were infectious diseases such as tuberculosis, smallpox, influenza, diphtheria, and polio. People of all social and economic levels and all age groups were susceptible to these diseases. However, with the development of vaccines and antibiotics, many of these diseases became much less life-threatening. For example, small pox has been virtually eradicated from most areas of the world as a result of a rigorous vaccination program.

The greatest threats to the health of Americans today are noninfectious diseases—lifestyle diseases such as cardiovascular disease and cancer. Among children injuries claim more lives than disease. The factors that determine the length and quality of an individual's life are most often personal choices in several areas: diet, exercise, and personal cleanliness; the use of tobacco, alcohol, and other drugs; and the application of new health information to one's own habits. Responsibility for maintaining health and for minimizing the risk of developing chronic and degenerative diseases and disorders rests with the individual and begins early in life. The role of health education is to promote positive attitudes, consistent positive behaviors, and good decision-making skills, which will contribute to good health and long-range prevention of disease. Research has shown that health education is more effective when content is aligned with skills practice. Skills practice challenges students to use their knowledge about health in their daily lives. Health education is really life education. *Your Health* provides rich skills practice throughout as skills are applied to everyday life activities students may encounter.

National Health Education Standards

The National Health Education Standards were developed in the 1990s with input from health professionals, educators, parents, and other community members. The standards provide a framework schools can use to enable their students to be healthy and successful.

According to the Joint Committee on National Health Education Standards, health literacy is the capacity of individuals to obtain, interpret, and understand basic health information and services and the competence to use such information and services in ways that enhance health. The National Health Education Standards address the ways in which health literacy is imparted.

Health Education Standard 1:
Students will comprehend concepts related to health promotion and disease prevention.

Health Education Standard 2:
Students will demonstrate the ability to access valid health information and health-promoting products and services.

Health Education Standard 3:
Students will demonstrate the ability to practice health-enhancing behaviors and reduce health risks.

Health Education Standard 4:
Students will analyze the influence of culture, media, technology, and other factors on health.

Health Education Standard 5:
Students will demonstrate the ability to use interpersonal communication skills to enhance health.

Harcourt Brace School Publishers

Health Education Standard 6:
Students will demonstrate the ability to use goal-setting and decision-making skills to enhance health.

Health Education Standard 7:
Students will demonstrate the ability to advocate for personal, family, and community health.

Developing Health Awareness

Many daily behaviors are health-related. Some of these behaviors, such as washing hands before meals and putting away supplies after work, occur in school as well as outside it. Other behaviors, such as crossing a street safely and playing safely, occur primarily outside of school. Some behaviors protect the health of the individual performing the behavior. Other behaviors protect all members of the group in which the individual functions. Through heightened awareness of the many daily behaviors that are health-related, students may become better equipped to apply these behaviors to their daily lives and to develop lasting good health habits.

Research shows that most students in health-oriented schools are better at practicing healthful behaviors such as avoiding the use of tobacco, alcohol, and other drugs; wearing safety belts; exercising regularly; and having regular checkups than their counterparts in other schools. By promoting a healthful lifestyle, health-oriented schools can play a significant role in reducing students' risk of developing chronic diseases. Focusing instruction to help students establish healthful lifestyles is an important part of health education.

Recognizing Stress and Emotional Crises

Teachers often have a better perspective on students' normal behavior and uniqueness than even their family members have. Teachers spend so much time with their students and get to know them so well that they can recognize behavioral changes when they occur. You notice when a student who has always been outgoing suddenly becomes sullen and clinging. You notice when a student you could always count on for a good-morning smile suddenly avoids looking at you. You know something is wrong when a student who has always been self-assured bursts into tears. These and other abrupt behavioral changes can signal that students are experiencing stress or facing emotional crises. How can you, in your role as a teacher, help your students cope with the difficult situations they experience?

Stress

Stress is a part of everyday life. Stress, in student as in adults, may manifest itself in many ways.

Physical signs of stress include
- unusually cold hands.
- ongoing muscle tension.
- fidgeting or twitching.
- playing with objects such as pens, pencils, and paper.
- distractibility or hyperactivity.
- tiredness.
- headaches.
- stomachaches.
- diarrhea.

Psychological signs of stress include
- fearfulness.
- suspicion. ("You are out to get me!")
- defensiveness. ("Why did you ask me that question?")

Symptoms of stress can sometimes be confused with symptoms resulting from problems related to medication, food allergies, or diet. If you suspect that medicine or diet is causing a student's behavior problems, you may want to consult with the school nurse or with the student's parents. You might share your observations with them and learn sufficient information from them to handle the situation.

School-Related Stress

Many school-related situations can cause stress for students. Occasionally, stress can become severe or chronic. Situations in which students are called upon to perform individually are typically stress producing. Taking tests, for example, can evoke a crippling fear of failure or of not meeting the expectations of self, friends, or parents. To students suffering from performance anxieties, reading aloud or otherwise performing in front of the class can be a traumatic experience.

If you recognize that students are experiencing excessive stress, you can help by giving them added reinforcement and encouragement and by using less stressful ways of evaluating their achievement levels. For example, students may not have to work at the board or to speak or read aloud in front of the class in order for you to make evaluations. Some students may learn better vicariously and perhaps perform better in small groups or on a one-to-one basis.

If test taking is a problem, reassure students that you realize they know more than the test results indicate. Temporarily allow such students to provide answers orally on a one-to-one basis to help remove the fear of testing. You can also let students know that although test taking is part of school, it is not the sole purpose of

Harcourt Brace School Publishers

school. Often you can reduce stress by encouraging students to relax and by assuring them that you are there to help. If the problem continues, you may want to consult with parents or guardians and with professionals in the school about stress-management strategies students could learn, such as relaxation techniques.

Stress from Peer Rejection

Students can be cruel at times in the feelings they express to one another. Peer rejection and the fear of peer rejection are common sources of stress in school. In this area your insight, perceptions, and gentle suggestion can be helpful. Sometimes students are rejected because their behavior is disruptive or because they are oblivious to the feelings and concerns of others. You can help by pointing out to these students why their behavior causes the reaction it does. If the situation is severe, you may want to talk to the student's parents or guardians and suggest that they involve the student in some community groups outside the classroom to help build confidence in relating to others.

One of the most devastating forms of peer rejection is being made a scapegoat by classmates. In such situations you may need to involve both the group and the student. Students need to understand that cruelty is unacceptable under any circumstances. You cannot make students like each other, but you can insist that they treat each other with respect, courtesy, and kindness.

You might also have a student who is experiencing rejection work with one of the more accepting students in the class. Often classmates will begin to accept a student when they realize that he or she has something to contribute. In addition, some warranted classroom praise, when appropriate, can help a student who is viewed by classmates as having nothing worthwhile to contribute. You may also want to talk with a school guidance counselor or with other teachers who know the student to determine areas in which she or he could excel in front of the class.

School Phobia and Stress

One kind of behavior that sometimes occurs as a reaction to stress or crisis has been termed *school phobia*. School phobia manifests itself when students simply refuse to attend school or go to school but soon feel ill and need to return home. Such behavior may even occur in students who have previously had excellent attendance records. Often these students will make up excuses for not going to school, such as a sore throat, an upset stomach, or a headache. In severe cases you may need to consult parents or guardians and a guidance counselor in order to shape students' behavior so they can go to school.

Often teachers, parents, or guardians assume that school-phobic behavior is the result of some unpleasantness in the classroom, and indeed this may be true. If the classroom environment is painful for a student, as in the case of peer rejection, then the student may exhibit school-phobic behaviors. More often than not, however, school phobia is an indication that there is an emotional crisis at home. For example, a student who flatly refuses to go to school may do so because he or she seldom sees the working parent and wants to spend more time at home. The illness of a family member, an impending divorce, or the occurrence of physical or emotional abuse at home may cause a student to exhibit school-phobic behavior.

When school phobia is the result of a crisis at home, you can help the family by encouraging the student to attend school. Helping such students focus on school activities will make remaining in school through the day easier.

Harcourt Brace School Publishers

Television and Stress

The effects of television programming on students has been the subject of much study and discussion. In addition to seeing extensive violence of many prime-time programs and cartoons, many students are exposed to evening news programs in which war, disease, crime, and child abuse are common topics. Young students know these things are bad but have no way of evaluating or coping with them. They may experience a quiet fear that can be quite stressful, if not traumatic. You can help students who are experiencing such stress and anxiety by providing a classroom environment that represents security and stability.

Emotional Crises in Students

The most common reaction children have to emotional crises is depression. Depression may manifest itself in a variety of behaviors, most often in withdrawal and sadness. Instead of withdrawing, however, some students may become hyperactive. They may be unable to sit still and may often cause disruption in the classroom and during breaks and between classes.

Another way a student may cope with an emotional crisis is by acting unusually happy, essentially denying the event or the importance of the event that underlies the crisis. Adults observing such behavior may wonder how the student can be so happy when a serious or even tragic event has occurred.

Students may also react to emotional crises with aloofness or aggressive behavior. These feelings may be accompanied by changes in interest levels. For example, some students may lose interest in school, whereas others may immerse themselves in school activities. Some students may become apathetic, whereas others may become perfectionists. Perfectionists may seem sad when their work is not perfect, as if

thinking, "I've already lost something very important to me. If my work isn't perfect, I may lose my teacher, too. I can't afford to do that."

Some students simply will not or cannot admit their feelings about events that are causing them emotional pain. As a result, they may look for outsiders to blame. Comments such as "I can't do my schoolwork because he is bothering me." are not uncommon. These may be clues that the student is reacting to a crisis outside the classroom.

In general, be observant of behavior changes in your students. Recognize that a change may not necessarily lead to a new kind of behavior; it may instead be an exaggerated form of an existing behavior. For example, a withdrawn student may become even more withdrawn, crying, giving up on friends, or not participating in school activities.

Some Common Causes of Emotional Crises

A list of all the emotional crises that students might have to confront would be very long. Students, after all, confront many of the same problems in daily life that adults face. The death of a friend or family member, divorce, and serious illness are emotionally wrenching for both adults and children and can ignite emotional crises in an individual of any age. However, young people often view changes in their environment differently than adults do and often have different ways of coping with changes.

Death

The way students perceive death varies with developmental age, experience, and family influences. As a result, students in your classroom who experience losses through death may react in different ways. A student may feel anger toward the person who died, thinking, "How could my mother be so mean as to leave us!" or "My mother didn't like me or she wouldn't have left." Later this anger may turn into guilt, with the student feeling, "If only I had been good, this wouldn't have happened."

Students also may be afraid of losing someone else. In a severe case, a student may refuse to come to school for fear the remaining parent will die while he or she is away. Some students may even be embarrassed about death and not want to talk about it with anyone. Other students may want everyone at school to know what happened before they return.

As a teacher you can provide an empathetic environment for students who have lost parents or other loved ones. Let students know that you are available to listen and, if possible, to help them express their feelings. Like adults, students go through a period of grieving. Be sure they know that it is normal to feel sad and to cry. If students are receptive, ask what they would like you to do. Some students may want you to speak to the class about what happened; others may prefer that you not mention the death at all. If a student seems very upset, you may wish to talk to adult family members or get professional advice from appropriate school personnel.

Remember that in situations such as these, the school may temporarily represent the only stability in the student's life. As such, the school environment can help students reestablish their daily routine. What students need most is the understanding and security that you provide just by being "teacher."

Divorce

According to the US Department of Health and Human Services, almost half the marriages in the United States end in divorce. Most classrooms have students from single-parent homes or from homes in which separation or divorce is being considered. Separation and divorce represent a

kind of collapse in a student's world. It may take even a mature student several years to come to terms with parental divorce.

Students often react to divorce with regressive behavior. They may become more juvenile, demanding greater and greater attention from those around them. Youngsters with divorced parents realize that something has happened, but they are unable to conceptualize it. As a result, they may feel insecure. One way they cope is by seeking more attention from adults.

Students often feel a profound sadness at the breakup of their parents' marriages. This sadness may be a deep depression with bouts of crying, especially if students are unable to express their feelings. Students may yearn for the parent who has left and at the same time feel angry at the parent for leaving. They may be angry with the parent who has remained at home, feeling that somehow this parent forced the other to leave.

Some students tend to take divorce calmly— at least outwardly. They may try to figure out why the divorce took place and then try to cope with their feelings about it. Their coping strategies may include participating more aggressively in activities outside the home, including schoolwork and extracurricular activities. Those students who are more aware of social expectations are often embarrassed by a divorce. They worry about their "image"—how they appear to other people. These students may try to bring their parents back together. When that fails, they may express disenchantment with the world as a whole and may feel a great deal of anger toward one or both parents.

As a teacher you may become an even more important adult in your students' lives as they confront emotional crises. You can provide a sustained interest in students, which they may not temporarily be receiving from any other source. You can also provide acceptance and support.

Harcourt Brace School Publishers

Remember, however, that you are not a counselor. It is not your responsibility to become students' surrogate parent, nor would it benefit them. You provide the greatest help by maintaining the classroom as a stable factor in students' lives.

Serious Illness

A serious illness in a family can create many of the same perceptions and reactions in students as a death can. Students may feel anger at first and then guilt and responsibility for the illness. Students even may be embarrassed by family members who are "different" and treat illnesses as secrets. They may be afraid that they or other family members will become ill. They may fear the person who is ill will die.

As a teacher you can provide students with additional support to help them through difficult times. Let students know that you are interested in what is happening. You may, for instance, ask how family members are doing, leaving the door open for further discussion. Let students know that you care what happens to them, and allow the stability of the classroom to provide a degree of emotional support.

Relocation

In order for a family member to attain certain career goals, it is often necessary for his or her family to move from one city to another. Relocation can be traumatic for students. In general, the more times students have experienced relocation, the greater the trauma. Students may feel that their world is unstable and that they are not in control of their environment. As a result, they may be less willing to invest in their environment by way of forming new relationships and getting involved in school activities. The more supportive the students' families are,

the better the students will be able to cope with these crises.

You can help new students adjust to the new environment by providing support and interest. Introduce new students to classmates you know to be friendly and open. In time new students should be able to trust in the stability of your classroom and find new friends.

Child Abuse

Whether emotional, physical, or sexual, child abuse is one of the most difficult problems with which you and your school administration may have to cope. In cases of abuse students' family members may not be advocates for the students' best interests. When a student is being abused emotionally, that is, when a student is subjected by family members to recurring cruel emotional situations, you may notice behavioral patterns such as extreme withdrawal, hyperactivity, or uncontrollable crying. These may all be clues that a student is suffering emotional abuse at home. The student may also display cruelty. Withdrawal, embarrassment, and a reluctance to speak about home or family members are typical of students suffering sexual and other kinds of physical abuse. However, signs of sexual abuse may not be as evident as signs of other physical abuse, such as repeated and unexplainable cuts, abrasions, and bruises.

If you suspect that a student in your classroom is being abused, you **must** report your suspicions to the proper school authority. **Do not take action on your own.** The school has the responsibility to follow up on your report, if necessary by calling the state division of youth and family services or another appropriate state agency. **Child abuse is a crime and must be handled within the confines of state guidelines.** Your role as a teacher is that of a referral

Harcourt Brace School Publishers

source, not a state investigator or a therapist. Outside the classroom there is little you can do. Within the classroom you provide a stable, safe environment—perhaps the only one in an abused student's life.

The Teacher's Role in Emotional Crises

As you cope with the stresses and crises of the students you teach, try to be an insightful and sensitive observer. You know your students' behavior patterns; you know when those patterns change. You also know that a change can signal a problem. Instead of showing anger or annoyance, attempt to find an opportunity to speak to the student. You might begin by saying, "I've noticed that you don't seem to be as cheerful as you usually are. I'm wondering if there is something wrong. Maybe there is something I can do to help." Let students know that you are there for them to talk to. If a student does not respond to your overtures, be careful not to force the issue; let the student bring it up. Be sensitive to a student's later acceptance of your invitation to talk about problems.

If a student seems unresponsive to your overtures and you remain concerned, you might share your observations and concerns with the student's parents or guardians. Depending on their reactions, you may want to suggest that they consult a counselor or a trained mental health practitioner. Remember that your role is to identify a student's personal problem, not to try to solve it. Trying to solve a problem can add to or create new ones. Classroom problems can be complex, and good solutions may be hard to find. An initial solution is often successful to a point, but it may require continued observation and creativity to prevent further problems.

A teacher cannot be a psychologist, a counselor, or a therapist. However, the sustained interest you exhibit in your students may, for some of them, be the one stabilizing factor in their lives. As adults we often remember our teachers even though we remember very few other adults from the time when we were in school. That in itself says something about the important role you, as a teacher, play in the lives of you students. Students need a structured environment in which they can experience learning along with a sense of caring and security. They need to know that someone expects them to do their very best without added pressure of emotional exceptions. Within the school setting that someone is you!

Coping with the Stress of Teaching

Although teaching can be very rewarding, it can also be stressful. When you recognize the degree of stress you experience, you can work to manage it. Just as you observe behavioral changes that indicate stress in students, you may notice changes in yourself that indicate stress, such as a racing heart, a headache, sweating, or jumpiness. Changes in eating and sleeping patterns can also signal undue stress. Are you drinking more coffee than usual? Are you eating more or less than usual? Do you crave particular kinds of foods? Are you having trouble sleeping? Are you waking up tired?

Your behavior toward others can also signal that you are under stress. Are you short-tempered? Do you seem to have less patience than usual with those around you? If you have children of your own, ask friends or family members how you are acting as a parent. If you suspect you are reacting to stress, confide in a friend. Ask if your friend has observed any behavioral changes in you.

Some simple techniques can help you relieve minor stress-related symptoms. One technique is to take a deep breath, hold it for a few seconds, and release it very slowly. Repeat the procedure several times. During school breaks, try to talk about nonschool subjects. You might want to learn more about meditation. Some people find meditating once or twice a day helps them control stress. Others use a planned exercise program or yoga to help them relax. You are not the only one suffering from stress. Some of your colleagues may also be experiencing many of the same symptoms. Perhaps some of them would be interested in participating in a support group.

If you feel unable to manage the stress on your own, ask your physician to recommend a mental health practitioner. Or ask about training in stress-management techniques such as biofeedback—a conditioning strategy that helps a person "listen" for the body's stress signals and then do something to reduce them. These techniques require some investment of time and money but are often beneficial.

If none of these measures provides relief, you may have reached what some call the "burned-out" stage. In that case you may want to consider more significant departures from your routine. For example, don't teach summer school. Do something entirely different for those months. Consider taking a sabbatical year to give yourself a rest and some time to reevaluate your goals.

As a teacher you are one of our country's most valuable resources. You are a leader of the nation's future. As such, your health—physical, intellectual, social, and emotional—is no less significant than the health of those you lead.

Harcourt Brace School Publishers

Diseases and Disorders: Background, Symptoms, and Classroom Implications

The following information about various infectious and noninfectious diseases and disorders is provided for your reference. Background information, symptoms, and classroom implications are given for each disease. Be sure to consult your school nurse or another medical authority if you have any questions or concerns about the health of your students.

Infectious Diseases and Disorders	Noninfectious Diseases and Disorders
Chicken Pox	Anorexia Nervosa
Colds	Appendicitis
Conjunctivitis (Pinkeye)	Asthma
Fifth Disease	Bronchitis (asthmatic or allergic)
Hepatitis	Cerebral Palsy (CP)
Human Immunodeficiency Virus (HIV) Infection and Acquired Immunodeficiency Syndrome (AIDS)	Diabetes
	Down Syndrome
Impetigo	Epilepsy
Influenza	Hearing Loss
Measles (Rubella, or German Measles)	Heart Disorders
	Hemophilia
Measles (Rubeola)	Leukemia
Mononucleosis (Mono)	Muscular Dystrophy
Mumps	Peptic Ulcer
Pediculosis (Lice)	Pleurisy
Pneumonia	Reye's Syndrome
Ringworm	Rheumatic Fever
Scabies	Rheumatoid Arthritis
Staphylococcal Infections (Staph)	Scoliosis
Strep Throat	Sickle-Cell Anemia
Sty	Tendinitis
Tonsillitis	Tetanus (Lockjaw)
Tuberculosis (TB)	Vision Disorders

Infectious Diseases and Disorders

Chicken Pox

Background: Chicken pox is caused by the Herpes zoster virus. This virus, in its reactivation stage, also causes shingles. Chicken pox is a relatively mild disease in normal children. However, Reye's syndrome, which has a relatively high fatality rate, is often preceded by chicken pox (see "Reye's syndrome" under "Noninfectious Diseases and Disorders"). A vaccine is now available for general use.

Symptoms: mild headache and moderate fever, a rash progressing to itching blisters containing clear fluid, scabs that are left when the blisters heal

Classroom Implications: Chicken pox is highly contagious and is spread by direct contact and through nasal discharge. Students who have had chicken pox may return to school when all the blisters have crusted over.

Colds

Background: Colds are caused by viruses. More than a hundred such viruses have been found to produce the inflammatory reactions associated with colds. Recovery does not produce a naturally acquired immunity. Therefore, attacks can occur as many as four or five times a year. Predisposing factors include excessive fatigue, allergic disorders, inhalation of noxious fumes, and other factors not yet identified. Becoming chilled does not, by itself, induce a cold.

Symptoms: a tickling sensation in the nose and throat, bouts of sneezing, watery nasal discharge, dulled senses of taste and smell, body aches, slight fever

Classroom Implications: Because cold and influenza viruses are highly infectious, a child with a "blossoming" cold should probably not be in school. However, many students do attend school while sick with colds. Reviewing basic hygiene with students, such as washing the hands regularly and covering the mouth when coughing or sneezing, may prevent the spread of the disease. Remember that a student with a cold does not function at optimum level in the classroom.

Conjunctivitis (Pinkeye)

Background: Conjunctivitis can be caused by viruses and bacteria or by allergies. Conjunctivitis is an inflammation of the membrane that covers the cornea or sclera (the white of the eye). Failure to obtain appropriate treatment can cause corneal scarring, which may lead to visual impairment.

Symptoms: pink or red sclera, possibly discharge or crust on the eyelids, itching, pain in the eyes

Classroom Implications: Conjunctivitis, other than allergic conjunctivitis, is highly contagious. A student suspected of having the disease should be referred to the school nurse immediately. Anyone having physical contact with the child's belongings should wash his or her hands thoroughly.

Fifth Disease

Background: Fifth disease is a mild illness caused by a virus, but if a pregnant woman gets the disease, it can infect the unborn child and may cause death to the fetus. The disease occurs most commonly in elementary school age children.

Symptoms: light red rash on the face and possibly also on the backs of the arms and legs that tends to come and go

Classroom Implications: Because fifth disease, although highly contagious, is relatively

Harcourt Brace School Publishers

harmless in children, children may not have to be kept out of school.

Hepatitis

Background: Hepatitis is a viral infection that causes inflammation of the liver. There are three types. Hepatitis A is spread through fecal contamination of water and food. Hepatitis B is spread through blood transfusions and the sharing of dirty needles by drug abusers. Hepatitis C is the most common from of hepatitis spread by blood transfusions. A vaccine is available for hepatitis A and hepatitis B.

Symptoms: nausea, vomiting, fever, loss of appetite during the early phase; jaundice, characterized by dark urine and yellowing of the body surfaces and the whites of the eyes, during the middle phase (after three to ten days)

Classroom Implications: Though hepatitis resolves itself within six to twelve weeks, it is a serious and debilitating illness. It is not generally thought that school exposure merits prophylactic gamma globulin injections. If more than one student in a class contracts hepatitis A, which is most common in children and young adults, it may be prudent to ask about the benefit of obtaining gamma globulin injections for the rest of the class. These injections provide some short-term protection against the virus. Good personal hygiene also helps prevent the spread of the disease and should be emphasized. A student who misses school because of hepatitis will most likely require home teaching until recovery is complete.

Human Immunodeficiency Virus (HIV) Infection and Acquired Immunodeficiency Syndrome (AIDS)

Background: HIV is the virus that causes AIDS. Most people with HIV infection develop AIDS.

The virus attacks the body's immune system, and infected people become susceptible to a variety of diseases that are usually not serious threats to people with normal immune systems. The AIDS diagnosis is determined by the presence of these infections and by blood tests. HIV is transmitted through contact with specific body fluids, including blood, semen, and vaginal secretions. It is not spread through the air, water, food, eating utensils, or skin to skin contact. Although there is no known cure for HIV infection, early diagnosis and new drug treatments may reduce the risk of developing life-threatening infections.

Symptoms: nonspecific symptoms such as swollen lymph glands, loss of appetite, chronic diarrhea, weight loss, fever and fatigue; viral and bacterial infections and cancers such as Karposi's sarcoma

Classroom Implications: Most districts have policies and procedures to protect against infection. Most people can avoid exposure to HIV by avoiding risky behaviors such as unprotected sex and sharing needles. District policy should include guidelines to prevent blood-to-blood transmission.

Impetigo

Background: Impetigo is a skin infection seen mostly in children. It is usually caused by streptococcal or staphylococcal bacteria. The infection usually appears on the legs, arms, or face and is treated with antibiotics.

Symptoms: yellow, honey-colored crusts; small blisters with pus; weeping sores; itching

Classroom Implications: Impetigo may be spread to others, though this has not been clearly proven. Students who have unexplained sores should be referred to the school nurse. Untreated lesions may persist for months and may cause scarring. Secondary infections in other parts of the body are possible. Students should be reminded to wash their hands and keep their fingernails clean.

Influenza

Background: The most frequent cause of influenza is the influenza A virus. It is spread by person-to-person contact and by droplets that have become airborne due to coughing, sneezing, or talking. Major epidemics occur about every three years and affect persons of all ages. Influenza is most prevalent in school children. The very young, the aged, and the infirm are at the greatest risk of developing complications from it. Each year a vaccine is formulated to protect against the flu viruses expected to circulate the following winter. Those at greatest risk of complications should receive the vaccine.

Symptoms: chills, fever, body aches and pains, headache, sore throat, cough, fatigue

Classroom Implications: Influenza is a self-limiting disease, with acute illness lasting for two to three days. Weakness and fatigue may persist for several days or occasionally for weeks. When a student returns to class after a bout with influenza, he or she may temporarily lack the ability to concentrate.

Measles (Rubella, or German Measles)

Background: Rubella is caused by a virus and is spread through personal contact and through airborne droplets. Rubella is milder and less contagious than rubeola, another type of measles. However, a pregnant woman who contracts rubella risks serious injury to the fetus.

Symptoms: a rash that eventually covers the body, lasting about three days; mild fever; tenderness and swelling of the lymph nodes at the back of the neck

Classroom Implications: Prevention of rubella has been a major health priority. All children should be vaccinated at fifteen months of age with a combination measles-mumps-rubella (MMR) vaccine.

Measles (Rubeola)

Background: Rubeola is caused by a virus that is spread by nose, throat, and mouth droplets. It is most contagious two to four days before the rash begins and during the acute phase. Though the vaccine for the prevention of measles has been available since 1963, a significant number of cases still occur each year. All children should be vaccinated against rubeola. The recommended age for inoculation is fifteen months and not before twelve months. The combined measles-mumps-rubella (MMR) vaccine is used.

Symptoms: hacking cough, sneezing, nasal discharge, redness of the eyes, sensitivity to light, fever, a rash beginning with spots in the mouth opposite the first and second molars

Classroom Implications: All children should be vaccinated against rubeola before entering school. All rubeola cases should be reported to the proper health authorities.

Mononucleosis (Mono)

Background: Infectious mononucleosis is caused by the Epstein-Barr virus, which is one of the herpes group of viruses. Mono is often called the "kissing disease," because it is spread by the oral-respiratory route. Mono is not very contagious. It may be positively diagnosed by a blood test.

Symptoms: fatigue, headache, chills, followed by high fever, sore throat, swelling of the lymph nodes, enlargement of the spleen

Classroom Implications: Infection with the Epstein-Barr virus occurs commonly in young people and often goes unrecognized, as it resembles a bad cold. Infectious mononucleosis, as described above, is predominantly a disease of adolescents and young adults. Symptoms can last weeks, and a variety of complications can occur. Many students with mono are out of school a long time and may be easily fatigued when they return, which should be taken into consideration in the classroom.

Mumps

Background: Mumps is caused by a virus that is spread by droplet infection or by materials that have been in contact with the infected saliva. The virus predominantly affects the parotid salivary glands, which are located in the cheek area, in front of the ears. When infected, these glands swell, giving the person a chipmunk-like appearance. Occasionally, the salivary glands under the tongue may become involved, and the neck area may swell.

Symptoms: chills, headache, loss of appetite, fever, pain when chewing or swallowing

Classroom Implications: All children should be vaccinated against mumps before entering school. The vaccine is usually given in a combined form with the measles and rubella vaccines. All mumps cases should be reported to the proper health authorities.

Pediculosis (Lice)

Background: Lice are small parasitic insects. Three types of lice can live on a human host. Crab lice (Phthirus pubis) are usually transmitted sexually. Body lice (Pediculus humanus corporis) are uncommon under good hygienic conditions. Head lice (Pediculus humanus capitis) are transmitted by personal contact and are common among school children regardless of personal hygiene. Head lice invade the scalp but can also move to the eyebrows, eyelashes, and

other facial hair. The lice lay eggs, called nits, which are grayish white and can be seen adhered to the hair shafts. The nits mature in three to fourteen days.

Symptoms: severe itching, white nits (eggs) that are tightly adhered to the hair shafts

Classroom Implications: The sharing of combs, hats, and other personal objects increases the chance that louse infestations will spread. Students should be told that such objects should not be shared. If a student in class is found to have lice, the other students should be checked with a hand lens and a fine-toothed comb by a person trained to identify lice and nits. The lice and nits can be killed with specially medicated shampoo or creams. Infected students should be kept out of the classroom for 24 hours following the application of effective treatment.

Pneumonia

Background: Pneumonia is an acute infection of the lungs caused by bacteria or viruses. Pneumococcal pneumonia, the most common bacterial pneumonia, occurs most frequently in winter. The pneumococci enter the respiratory passages and lodge in the bronchial tubes, eventually making their way deep into the lungs. Pneumococcal pneumonia can be passed to other people, though it is not very contagious. A vaccine is available but is not commonly used except for patients who are debilitated or immunocompromised.

Symptoms: sudden onset, shaking chills, chest pain, cough, fever, headache

Classroom Implications: Many times pneumonia presents itself as a secondary infection. A child who has had influenza or an acute upper respiratory infection and then suddenly has a relapse should be taken to a physician immediately. Prompt antibiotic treatment is important and usually leads to a rapid recovery.

Ringworm

Background: Ringworm is a superficial skin infection caused by any of a number of fungi that invade only the dead tissue of skin. Infection by a certain fungus can produce raised rings on the skin, as if a worm had been at work (hence the name ringworm). However, many other fungi cause different symptoms. The various fungi attack specific areas of the skin.

Symptoms: slowly spreading, scaly, ring-shaped spots on the skin (ringworm of the body, *Tinea corporis*); scaling lesions between the toes (athlete's foot, *Tinea pedis*); thickened, luster-less nails with a darkened appearance (ring-worm of the nails, *Tinea unguium*); small, scaly lesions on the scalp and semibald, grayish patches with broken, lusterless hairs (ringworm of the scalp, *Tinea capitis*)

Classroom Implications: The most common of the ringworms are athlete's foot and ringworm of the scalp. Athlete's foot is often spread at swimming pools and in showers, locker rooms, and other such facilities used by many people. Ringworm of the scalp mainly affects children. If this condition is suspected, a student should immediately be referred to the school nurse.

Scabies

Background: Scabies is a infectious parasitic skin infection caused by the itch mite (Sarcoptes scabiei). Pregnant female mites tunnel into the skin and deposit their eggs. The larvae hatch after a few days and group around the hair follicles. Skin lesions form due to hypersensitivity to the parasites. Scabies is transmitted easily through skin-to-skin contact, often infecting entire households. It is not spread through clothing or bedding.

Symptoms: intense itching; burrows (fine, wavy, dark lines with small pimple-like lesions at the open ends) occurring commonly between the fingers; burrows also occurring on the insides of the wrists, around the elbows, around the aureolae of the breasts of females, on the geni-tals of males, along the belt line, and on the lower buttocks

Classroom Implications: Cases of scabies need to be referred to health professionals and treated immediately.

Staphylococcal Infections (Staph)

Background: Staphylococcal bacteria are com-monly found on the skin of many healthy adults. People who are hospitalized or work in hospitals have a slightly higher incidence of car-rying the penicillin-resistant strains. Staph food poisoning is caused by the toxin produced by the staphylococci in contaminated food.

Symptoms: fever, headache, boils, abscesses, skin lesions with pus

Classroom Implications: All staph infections should be treated promptly by a health professional.

Strep Throat

Background: Strep throat is caused by one form of streptococcal bacterium. A throat culture can confirm the presence of streptococcal bacteria.

Symptoms: sore, beefy-red throat; fever; swollen neck "glands"; occasionally, oozing from the tonsils

Classroom Implications: Delayed complications of strep throat can be life-threatening. Rheumatic heart disease may develop. Therefore, it is very important that students who show possible symptoms of the disease be diagnosed as soon as possible. Any student with severe sore throat that is not accompanied by a cough, laryngitis, or stuffy nose should be suspect.

Harcourt Brace School Publishers

Sty

Background: Sties are infections that form on the eyelids and are caused by staphylococcal bacteria that have made their way into the tiny glands in the area. There are two types of sties: external and internal. The external produces a painful, visible abscess that usually becomes pointed and then drains. An internal sty forms toward the eye and seldom erupts through the skin.

Symptoms: a small, yellowish spot accompanied by pain, redness, tenderness of the eyelid, sensitivity to light, the feeling of having a foreign body in the eye (external sty); pain, localized redness and swelling, abscess formation on the inside of the eyelid, and, rarely, spontaneous drainage (internal sty)

Classroom Implications: Students who develop sties should be referred to the school nurse for medical treatment.

Tonsillitis

Background: Tonsillitis is an acute inflammation of the tonsils, often caused by strepococcal bacteria. Less frequently, it is caused by a virus.

Symptoms: sore throat and pain, especially upon swallowing; high fever; body ache; headache; vomiting; oozing from the tonsils

Classroom Implications: Repeated tonsillitis may prevent a student from attending school for weeks at a time. Repeated attacks may signal the need for removal of the tonsils. When students return to school after tonsillectomies, there are usually few restrictions on their activity.

Tuberculosis (TB)

Background: Tuberculosis is an acute or chronic disease caused by a rod-shaped bacterium. TB is primarily a pulmonary disease but can strike many other organs and tissues in the body. Infection usually occurs through inhaling infectious droplets. The bacteria settle in the lower or middle section of the lungs and begin to multiply. The body's immune system then begins to fight the disease, producing antibodies against it. Infection may continue, or it may abate. If a latency period does occur, the bacteria may reactivate at any time. TB can be detected by a chest X ray, which can reveal a primary infection of the lungs, or by the tuberculin skin test or patch test.

Symptoms: fever, body aches, chronic cough that expels sputum

Classroom Implications: In the United States TB has re-emerged as a serious public health problem, affecting minorities disproportionately. Drug-resistant cases of TB have also increased dramatically. TB is primarily an airborne disease, and adequate ventilation is an important measure in preventing its transmission. Infected people who are symptom-free are not contagious.

Noninfectious Diseases and Disorders

Anorexia Nervosa

Background: Anorexia nervosa is an eating disorder that usually begins around the time of puberty. It is most common among adolescent girls. The disease is characterized by a distorted concept of body image and involves extreme weight loss. Many people with the disorder look emaciated but are convinced they are overweight. Bulimia nervosa is a variant of anorexia nervosa. It is characterized by eating binges followed by purges. Purging may involve vomiting, abusing laxatives or diuretics, taking enemas, exercising obsessively, or a combination of these. As body fat decreases, the menstrual cycle is interrupted.

Symptoms: rapid weight loss, change in eating habits, obsession with exercise to lose weight, increased use of laxatives, depressed mental state, cessation of menstruation, sores in or around the mouth from excessive forced vomiting

Classroom Implications: Eating disorders such as anorexia nervosa and bulimia nervosa may occur in both mild and severe forms. They are most successfully treated when diagnosed early. Many cases have been discovered by teachers, who have made appropriate referrals. Students with eating disorders need the emotional support and understanding of their teachers. Increased efforts to enhance self-concept in the classroom contribute greatly toward treatment goals.

Appendicitis

Background: Appendicitis is most common in adolescents and young adults but is also a major reason for abdominal surgery in children. The appendix becomes infected with bacteria normally found in the bowel. Continued inflammation may lead to abscess formation, gangrene, and perforation resulting in peritonitis.

Symptoms: steady, well-localized pain, usually in the lower right abdominal quadrant; constipation that began recently; nausea and vomiting; mild fever; elevated white blood cell count

Classroom Implications: A student returning to the classroom after an appendectomy may have restrictions on his or her activity for a time. The student may tire easily the first few days and have difficulty concentrating.

Asthma

Background: Asthma is a chronic lung condition that results in recurring attacks of breathing problems. Attacks can be triggered by upper respiratory infections (colds or flu); exercise; laughing or crying hard; allergies to common substances such as animal dander (tiny scales from skin), pollen, or dust; irritants such as cold air, strong smells, and chemical sprays (perfume, paint and cleaning solutions, chalk dust, lawn and turf treatments); weather changes; tobacco smoke. During an attack the muscles surrounding the bronchial tubes go into spasm, thus reducing the size of the airway. The allergic response causes mucus production and a resultant productive cough. People with asthma are able to draw air into the lungs through the narrowed airway but are unable to force carbon dioxide waste out. Victims may wheeze, gasp for air, and feel that they are suffocating.

Symptoms: wheezing, gasping for air, hacking cough, tightness in the chest, shortness of breath

Classroom Implications: An asthma attack may be compared to taking a deep breath and not being able to let it out. A student having an asthma attack should be reassured that help is on the way. People with asthma are often fearful of the attacks and may sometimes feel that they may lead to death. An attack may occur at any time and may be initiated by emotional strain, physical exertion, or environmental factors. Many students with asthma take prescription medicines, which should be available to them when needed. These medicines may cause jitteriness, overactivity, or, rarely, drowsiness. With modern medical management and close follow-up, students with asthma should usually have few restrictions on activity, except during or following an acute attack.

Bronchitis (asthmatic or allergic)

Background: Bronchitis is a secondary infection of the bronchial tubes. It may develop as a result of an upper respiratory infection. A virus or bacterium invades the area and causes an increase in inflammation and in mucus secretion. A deep,

Harcourt Brace School Publishers

rumbling cough develops. Treatment is directed at drainage and expulsion of the mucus rather than at suppression of the cough.

Symptoms: chills, slight fever, back and muscle pain, sore throat, followed by dry cough and then by a cough that expels mucus

Classroom Implications: Bronchitis is a self-limiting disease in most cases; complete healing usually occurs within a few weeks. The student who has bronchitis, however, may be absent for a time and may require help in making up missed work.

Cerebral Palsy (CP)

Background: Cerebral palsy is a term for a group of motor disorders that impair voluntary movement. The various forms of CP are caused by damage to the central nervous system before, during, or soon after birth. Physical therapy helps many children with CP overcome their disabilities.

Symptoms: spasticity of limbs, weakness, limb deformities, speech disorders, involuntary movements, difficulty with fine movements, visual disturbances; commonly accompanied by nerve deafness, mental impairment, or seizure disorders.

Classroom Implications: Students with severe CP are usually not mainstreamed. However, in mild forms of CP, the symptoms may be seen only during certain activities, such as running. Students with mild CP have normal intelligence and usually function well in a regular classroom setting. Be aware of a CP student's particular needs, and try to smooth the way for including the student in classroom activities. Discussing the disorder with classmates and explaining why the student may sometimes move differently will increase understanding and help eliminate teasing.

Diabetes

Background: Diabetes is characterized by an increase of sugar in the blood and urine. In the pancreas, cell groups known as the islets of Langerhans fail to secrete adequate amounts of the hormone insulin. Insulin is the primary substance that allows the body to utilize sugar. In most cases there is a genetic predisposition to develop diabetes. There is no known cure. Optimal treatment usually consists of regulated insulin replacement, diet, and exercise.

Symptoms: frequent urination, thirst, hunger, weight loss

Classroom Implications: Teachers are often in a position to help identify diabetics who have not yet been diagnosed. Any changes in bathroom or drinking habits should be investigated. A sudden weight loss or the inability to concentrate should also be suspect. A student with regulated diabetes functions normally in the classroom. If you have a diabetic student requiring insulin shots, keep a source of sugar, such as orange juice, available for insulin-shock emergencies. You may also need to accommodate a diabetic student who must have a snack once or several times a day.

Down Syndrome*

Background: Down syndrome is an inherited condition that is usually associated with an extra chromosome. Fifty percent of infants with the syndrome are born to mothers over the age of 35. Children with Down syndrome have a mean IQ of 50. They usually have small heads and slanted eyes. Life expectancy is normal in the absence of other birth defects.

Symptoms: placidity, failure to cry (infants), lack of muscle tone; slanted eyes, flattened nosebridge; mouth usually held open because of enlarged tongue; short-fingered, broad hands

Harcourt Brace School Publishers

with single crease; feet with a wide gap between the first and second toes.

Classroom Implications: Children with Down syndrome are often placed in special classes that can meet their unique needs. But many students with special needs are part of the regular classroom community. Their classmates need to develop an understanding of the conditions that make others different. A careful introduction to disabilities is a must for the whole class.

* *Genetic conditions named for individuals are spelled without 's, as recommended by the American Society of Human Genetics.*

Epilepsy

Background: Epilepsy, a disorder of the nerve cells in the brain, is characterized by attacks called seizures. The three well-known kinds of seizures are called grand mal, petit mal, and psychomotor. During a seizure brain impulses become chaotic, causing the person to lose consciousness and control over body movement.

Symptoms: uncontrollable jerking movements followed by a deep sleep (grand-mal seizure); momentary cessation of movement (petit-mal seizure); coordinated but strange whole body movements (psychomotor seizure)

Classroom Implications: If a student has a grand-mal seizure, do not attempt to restrain the student. If the student has not fallen to the floor, place him or her on the floor and move furniture and other obstructions out of the way. Do not place any objects in the student's mouth. A convulsive seizure may be a frightening experience for classmates to witness, so offer them explanation and reassurance. Petit-mal seizures, though less dramatic than grand-mal seizures, make the student unresponsive; a student experiencing a petit-mal episode briefly loses consciousness. Anticonvulsive medication may slow down an epileptic student, occasionally making concentration difficult. Computer screens, video games, and flashing lights have been known to produce seizures. People with epilepsy are usually told to avoid heights.

Hearing Loss

Background: Many conditions can produce hearing loss. Conduction deafness can be caused by sound waves being blocked by wax or by scars from middle-ear infections. It can also be caused by Eustachian tube dysfunction, middle-ear fluid, or fixation of the bones of the middle ear. Most of these conditions can be reversed, and normal hearing can be restored. However, when the auditory nerve is damaged, little can be done.

Symptoms: frequent asking for repetition of what was said, frequent misunderstanding of verbal directions, failure to respond to normal voices or sounds, cupping of the ear to funnel sounds

Classroom Implications: Students with diagnosed hearing loss may require special learning aids in the classroom. Many students who have hearing loss need to wear one or two hearing aids, which should be explained to the rest of the class. Other supplemental amplification aids should be supplied when needed. If you observe changes in any student's ability to hear, make referrals for testing.

Heart Disorders

Background: Many conditions can cause heart disorders. The most common disorders in infancy and early childhood are congenital abnormalities such as valvular problems, holes between right and left chambers (septal defects), and failure of an opening between the aorta and pulmonary arteries to close after birth (a condition

Harcourt Brace School Publishers

called patent ductus arteriosus). These conditions can be surgically corrected in most instances. Another type of heart condition is a heart murmur, a series of prolonged heart sounds that can be heard as vibrations. Some murmurs are significant and others are not. Some significant murmurs may signal developmental heart-valve abnormalities. Those murmurs that are termed functional or insignificant usually resolve themselves as a youngster matures physically.

Symptoms: shortness of breath, chest pain, blue tinge to the skin, fatigue, slowing of heartbeat rate, palpitations.

Classroom Implications: Children who have had surgery for congenital heart disorders usually lead restriction-free lives. Those who have continuing problems or who develop additional problems may have to curtail physical activity, and you may need to make special plans for them. All students should be encouraged to develop good physical fitness habits and healthful eating habits to help protect them from heart disease in later life.

Hemophilia

Background: Hemophilia is an inherited bleeding disorder. The person is unable to manufacture certain essential clotting factors and therefore might bleed to death if a simple cut or bruise is left untreated.

Symptoms: serious bleeding or bruising from trivial injuries

Classroom Implications: Most students who have hemophilia can lead normal lives if they are receiving treatment for the missing blood-clotting factor. However, you should be aware of this condition and take necessary precautions to prevent injury. First-aid procedures for bleeding should be reviewed with the school nurse or with a physician.

Leukemia

Background: Some forms of leukemia in animals are caused by viruses, but a similar cause in humans has not been verified. Environmental factors such as radiation and chemical exposure may be contributory. There are several types of leukemia. Acute lymphoblastic leukemia (ALL) is a disease that primarily affects children. Acute myeloblastic leukemia (AML) can occur in people of any age. In all people with leukemia, abnormal white blood cells form in large numbers. These cells quickly invade many tissues, causing enlargement of organs, severe anemia, and bleeding.

Symptoms: high fever and joint pain; bleeding from the mouth, nose, kidneys, and large intestine; enlarged liver, spleen, and lymph nodes

Classroom Implications: Continual improvement in chemotherapy has made remissions (absences of any signs of the disease) much more common, especially in acute lymphoblastic leukemia. Students undergoing treatment for leukemia may be able to return to school after the acute stage of the disease has been arrested. However, depending on the treatment schedule, they may have to return to the hospital periodically. Every effort to maintain continuity in the classroom for these students should be made. Many of the drugs that are administered cause hair loss, which should be explained to the rest of the class. Sometimes students become frightened by the word cancer, and questions such as "Can I catch it?" "Will he die?" and "Will I die?" may be asked. Dealing with these types of concerns openly and honestly may alleviate fear and anxiety.

Muscular Dystrophy

Background: The muscular dystrophies are a group of inherited progressive diseases that produce a breakdown in the muscle fibers, causing increasing weakness and difficulty with movement. Duchenne muscular dystrophy is the most common form. It occurs in boys three to seven years of age. The disease causes a steady increase in muscle weakness, and most patients are confined to a wheelchair by age of ten or twelve.

Symptoms: muscle weakness causing a waddling gait, toe-walking, a swaybacked appearance, frequent falls, difficulty in standing up and in climbing stairs.

Classroom Implications: About 50 percent of the children with muscular dystrophy have lower-than-average IQs. Many have such a degree of debilitation that placement in regular classes would not be to their advantage. However, many children with muscular dystrophy, especially the less common milder forms, are mainstreamed. If one of your students has muscular dystrophy, you need to be aware of his of her limitations. Special equipment may be needed for instruction and for the comfort of the student. Fostering understanding among classmates is of utmost importance.

Peptic Ulcer

Background: A peptic (stomach) ulcer is a chronic disease that results from the overproduction of gastric juices manufactured by the stomach to break down foods. Sometimes the mechanism for secreting gastric juices does not shut off after the food has been digested, and the juices begin to break down the lining of the digestive tract itself. The size of peptic ulcers varies from a quarter inch to several inches in diameter. If untreated, peptic ulcers may reach deeper and deeper into the stomach wall until a large blood vessel is penetrated, causing massive hemorrhaging or complete perforation of the wall. Ulcer formation may be aggravated by smoking, coarse food, and stress. Peptic ulcers

are relatively common among adults, though they do occur in children, even before the age of ten.

Symptoms: a painful burning sensation, usually relieved by meals and occurring at night; nausea and vomiting if the pain is severe; constipation; anemia

Classroom Implications: Students who complain of persistent, localized stomach pain should see a physician. A supervised diet, antacids, bed rest, and avoidance of emotional upset are the favored treatment. If stress is determined to be the cause of the ulcer, you can help by providing ways for the student to experience less stress in school.

Pleurisy

Background: Pleurisy is an inflammation of the thin membrane that lines the chest cavity and covers the lungs. It usually occurs as a result of an infection in the lungs but can be caused by trauma to the membrane and by other factors.

Symptoms: sudden, intense, perhaps stabbing pain at the site of inflammation (in the chest, in or under the rib cage); pain aggravated by breathing or coughing

Classroom Implications: Depending on the cause of the disease, students who have had pleurisy may require restricted activity when they return to school. They may also require special help in making up missed work.

Reye's Syndrome

Background: The cause of Reye's syndrome is currently unknown. This illness often follows an acute viral infection (most commonly influenza or chicken pox), especially if aspirin was given to reduce fever. Reye's syndrome occurs in young people under the age of 18 and usually develops in the late fall or winter. The severity of the disease varies greatly. Fatality rates average 42 percent.

Symptoms: uncontrollable nausea and vomiting starting about the sixth day after a viral infection; noticeable change in mental function; lethargy, mild amnesia, disorientation, agitation, unresponsiveness, coma, seizures, fixed and dilated pupils

Classroom Implications: Parents should be informed of the possible link between aspirin and Reye's syndrome. The syndrome may leave permanent neurological damage, causing mental retardation or problems with movement.

Rheumatic Fever

Background: Rheumatic fever is a possible secondary complication of a streptococcal infection, especially strep throat. Rheumatic fever is an acute inflammatory reaction to the streptococcal bacterium and can affect one or more major sites, including the joints, the brain, the heart, and the skin. The disease is rare before four years of age and uncommon after age 18.

Symptoms: varied symptoms appearing alone or in combination after a severe sore throat; a flat, painless rash, lasting less than a day; painless nodules on the legs; swollen tender joints; recurrent fevers; movement disorders

Classroom Implications: Since rheumatic fever can develop to varying degrees, the amount of physical restriction that must be imposed after an attack depends on the cardiac problems of the individual. Psychological problems have been noted in students who have been restricted from play just because they have rheumatic fever. It is important for all parents and school personnel to see that a student with a possible strep infection is treated promptly. Any changes in a student's work habits, appearance, or energy level after a strep infection should be investigated.

Rheumatoid Arthritis

Background: Rheumatoid arthritis is a chronic disorder characterized by inflammation of the joints. In children the knees, elbows, wrists, and other large joints tend to be affected. This may result in interference with growth and development. In some cases the eyes and heart are affected. Complete remission is more likely in children than in adults.

Symptoms: rash, fever, inflammation of the irises, enlargement of the spleen and lymph nodes; swelling, pain, and tenderness of the involved joints

Classroom Implications: A student with rheumatoid arthritis may be absent frequently because of the chronic, recurring nature of the disease and may need help in keeping up with school work. Stiffness of joints and possible deformities may limit the student's movement. Caution should be exercised in lifting the student or pulling on affected limbs in any way. Restrictions on the student's activity can be less burdensome if you explain the situation to the whole class. Emotional support from classmates can contribute to the student's sense of well-being.

Scoliosis

Background: Scoliosis is a lateral curvature of the spine. This disorder occurs most commonly during the adolescent growth period. It is estimated that between 5 and 10 percent of school-age children have spinal curvatures in varying degrees. However, only about 2 percent of the cases are significant. The effect of scoliosis depends on its severity, how early it is detected, and how promptly it is treated. The malformation usually does not get worse once the spine has reached full growth. Scoliosis is more common among girls than boys.

Symptoms: unequal shoulder levels, a pronounced hunchbacked appearance, tiredness or muscle aches in the lower back region, persistent back pain

Classroom Implications: Many states now require scoliosis screening for preadolescent and adolescent students. Treatment of scoliosis may range from simple remedial exercises to corrective surgery. Special braces or casts may also be necessary, which can threaten a teenager's self-concept. Therefore, counseling and support from teachers, parents, and peers are very important in treating a youngster with scoliosis.

Sickle-Cell Anemia

Background: Sickle-cell anemia is an inherited disease that affects blacks almost exclusively. Anemias are conditions in which the blood is low in red blood cells or in hemoglobin, causing a decrease in the body's ability to transport oxygen to all cells. This disease is named after the abnormal, sickle shape of some red blood cells. Because of their shape these cells are not able to flow easily through the capillaries and tend to jam up around joints and in organs. This inhibiting of blood flow can cause acute pain.

Symptoms: severe anemia, fatigue, sickle-shaped red blood cells, moderate jaundice, enlarged spleen, poor body development

Classroom Implications: Sickle-cell anemia is a chronic disease that can cause repeated painful crisis situations that may require hospital treatment. A student with the disease may be out of school frequently and will need help in completing schoolwork and maintaining contact with

the class. As with all inherited diseases, genetic counseling is recommended.

Tendinitis

Background: Tendinitis is an inflammation of the tendons surrounding various joints. The inflammation usually results from a joint being forced beyond its normal range of motion or in an abnormal direction. Excessive exercise or repeated injury to a joint may also cause tendinitis. A common form of tendinitis, tennis elbow, results from the excessive rotation of the forearm and hand while playing tennis. The muscles of the forearm are strained, and the inflammation spreads to the elbow.

Symptoms: swelling, local tenderness, disabling pain when the affected joint is moved

Classroom Implications: Students may develop tendinitis from excessive periods of repeated exercise such as pitching a baseball or hitting a tennis ball. Students who spend many hours working the levers of video games may experience tendinitis of the wrist joint. Tendinitis may often be prevented through proper coaching in sports and appropriate periods of rest. Students who complain of constant, disabling pain in the shoulder, wrist, elbow, knee, or other joints should be referred to a physician.

Tetanus (Lockjaw)

Background: Tetanus is an acute infectious disease caused by a bacterium that produces spores and that can live in an environment without oxygen. The spores are found in soil and in animal feces. Once the toxin from the bacterium enters the body, it interferes with the central nervous system's ability to transmit impulses correctly. This causes a generalized spasticity and intermittent convulsive movements of the

Harcourt Brace School Publishers

body. Stiffness of the jaw is a classic symptom of tetanus (hence the name lockjaw). The typical route of transmission is through a skin wound, usually a puncture wound, that has been contaminated with dirt containing the spores. The spores then develop into bacteria that release the toxin. Primary immunization against tetanus should be done when a child is two months, four months, six months, and 15 to 18 months. This is given in the form of a DTP (diptheria-tetanus-pertussis) combination vaccine. After that, booster injections should be administered when needed, usually at about school age and then every ten years.

Symptoms: stiff jaw muscles and difficulty in swallowing; restlessness and irritability; stiffness in the neck, arms, or legs; headache, fever, sore throat, chills, convulsions

Classroom Implications: It is extremely important to clean all wounds promptly and thoroughly to prevent the development of tetanus. If a student suffers a severe wound and has not had a tetanus booster within five years, a booster should be given as soon as possible. All wound injuries should be reported to the school nurse for proper first aid and evaluation.

Vision Disorders

Background: There are three common eye disorders that produce errors in refraction and that decrease visual acuity. The most common disorder is farsightedness (hyperopia), which interferes with the ability to see clearly things that are nearby. In nearsightedness (myopia) a person is able to see things clearly that are near, but distance vision is impaired. Astigmatism, or distorted vision, occurs when there are defective curvatures of the refractive surfaces of the eye.

Symptoms: squinting, headaches, eye muscle fatigue, holding reading material unusually close or far away, complaining of not being able to see the chalkboard

Classroom Implications: Students with undiagnosed eye disorders may have a difficult time with schoolwork. As a teacher you are in an excellent position to note such problems and to make appropriate referrals.

Directory of Health Services and Agencies

The following directory can be helpful in your classroom planning and teaching activities. Many of the agencies listed will answer questions about specific health concerns and will provide written information upon request. Some of the organizations listed have state, county, or local offices. Hotline numbers and toll-free numbers and Internet addresses are supplied, if available. Please note that this information, while correct at time of publication, is subject to change.

Human Immunodeficiency Virus (HIV) Infection and AIDS (Acquired Immunodeficiency Syndrome)

American Red Cross National Headquarters
AIDS Education Office
8111 Gatehouse Rd. JP6
Falls Church, VA 22042
(703) 737-8300
Fax: (703) 206-7673
Internet Address: www.redcross.org

American Selfhelp Clearinghouse
N.W. Covenant Medical Center
25 Pocono Rd.
Denville, NJ 07834
(973) 625-3037
Internet Address: www.cmhc.com/selfhelp

CDC Public Health Services
(800) 342-AIDS
Internet Address: www.cdcnac.org

Alcohol Abuse

Al-Anon Family Group Headquarters
1600 Corporate Landing Parkway
Virginia Beach, VA 23454
(757) 563-1600
Fax: (757) 563-1655
Internet Address: www.al-anon.alateen.org

Mothers Against Drunk Driving (MADD)
511 E. John Carpenter Freeway, Suite 700
Irving, TX 75062
(214) 744-MADD
(800) 438-MADD
Internet Address: www.madd.org

National Commission Against Drunk Driving
1900 L St. N.W., Suite 705
Washington, DC 20036
(202) 452-6004
Fax: (202) 223-7012
Internet Address: www.ncadd.com

National Institute on Alcohol Abuse and Alcoholism
Willco Building
6000 Executive Blvd.
Bethesda, MD 20892-7003
(301) 443-3860
Internet Address: www.niaaa.nih.gov

Office of Substance Abuse Prevention
National Clearinghouse for Alcohol and Drug Information
P.O. Box 2345
Rockville, MD 20847-2345
(301) 468-2600
(800) 729-6686
Fax: (301) 468-6433
Internet Address: www.health.org

Students Against Driving Drunk (SADD)
P.O Box 800
Marlboro, MA 01752
(508) 481-3568
(800) 886-2972
Fax: (508) 481-5759
Internet Address: www.nat-sadd.org

Allergy

Asthma and Allergy Foundation of America
1125 15th St. N.W., Suite 502
Washington, DC 20005
(800) 727-8462
Internet Address: www.aafa.org

Arthritis

Arthritis Foundation
1330 West Peachtree St.
Atlanta, GA 30309
(404) 872-7100
Fax: (404) 872-0457
Internet Address: www.arthritis.org

Asthma

Asthma and Allergy Foundation of America
1125 15th St. N.W., Suite 502
Washington, DC 20005
(800) 727-8462
Internet Address: www.aafa.org

Harcourt Brace School Publishers

Cancer

American Cancer Society
1599 Clifton Rd. N.E.
Atlanta, GA 30329
(404) 320-3333
Internet Address: www.cancer.org

Leukemia Society of America, Inc.
600 Third Ave.
New York, NY 10016
(212) 573-8484
Fax: (212) 856-9686
Internet Address: www.Leukemia.org

National Cancer Institute
Cancer Information Service
9000 Rockville Pike
Bethesda, MD 20892
(800) 4-CANCER
Fax: (301) 402-5874
Internet Address: www.cancernet.nci.nih.gov

Child Abuse

Clearinghouse on Child Abuse and Neglect
P.O. Box 1182
Washington, DC 20013-1182
(703) 385-7565
Fax: (703) 385-3206
Internet Address: www.calib.com/nccanch

National Committee for the Prevention of Child Abuse
332 South Michigan Ave.
Suite 1600
Chicago, IL 60604
(312) 663-3520
Fax: (312) 939-8962
Internet Address: www.childabuse.org

Infectious Diseases

Centers for Disease Control and Prevention
1600 Clifton Rd. N.E.
Atlanta, GA 30333
(404) 639-3311
Internet Address: www.CDC.gov

Consumer Information

Consumer Education Research Center
1980 Springfield Ave.
Maplewood NJ 07040
(973) 275-3955
Fax: (973) 275-3980

Consumer Information Center
18th and F Streets N.W.
Washington, DC 20405
(202) 501-1794
Fax: (202) 501-4281
Internet Address: www.pueblo.gsa.gov

Consumer Product Safety Commission
Office of the Secretary
Washington, DC 20207
(800) 638-CPSC
Fax: (301) 504-0051
Internet Address: www.CPSC.gov

Council of Better Business Bureaus
4200 Wilson Blvd., Suite 800
Arlington, VA 22203-1838
(703) 276-0100
Internet Address: www.bbb.org

Cystic Fibrosis

Cystic Fibrosis Foundation
2250 N. Druid Hills Rd. N.W., Suite 275
Atlanta, GA 30329
(404) 325-6973
Internet Address: www.cff.org

Dental Health

American Dental Association
211 East Chicago Ave.
Chicago, IL 60611
(800) 621-8099
Internet Address: www.ada.org

American Dental Hygienist Association
444 North Michigan Ave., Suite 3400
Chicago, IL 60611
(800) 243-2342
Fax: (312) 440-8929
Internet Address: www.adha.org

Diabetes

American Diabetes Association
National Service Center
1660 Duke St.
Alexandria, VA 22314
(703) 549-1500
(800) 232-3472
Internet Address: www.diabetes.org

**Juvenile Diabetes Foundation
International Hotline**
120 Wall St.
New York, NY 10005
(212) 889-7575
(800) 223-1138
Internet Address: www.jdf.cure.com

Drug Abuse

**National Clearinghouse for Alcohol and
Drug Abuse Information**
P.O. Box 2345
Rockville, MD 20847-2345
(301) 468-2600
(800) 729-6686
Fax: (301) 468-6433
Internet Address: www.health.org

National Institute on Drug Abuse (NIDA)
5600 Fishers Lane
Room 10-05
Rockville, MD 20857
(301) 443-6480
Fax: (301) 443-9127

Eating Disorders

**American Anorexia/Bulimia
Association, Inc.**
165 W. 46th St.
1108
New York, NY 10036
(212) 575-6200
Internet Address:
    www.members.aol.com/AmAnBu

Environment

Environmental Protection Agency
Public Information Center
401 M Street S.W.
Washington, DC 20460
(202) 260-2090
Internet Address: www.epa.gov

General Health

**American Association for Health, Physical
Education, Recreation, and Dance**
1900 Association Dr.
Reston, VA 20191
(703) 476-3400
Fax: (703) 476-9527
Internet Address: www.aahperd.org

American School Health Association
7263 State Route 43
P.O. Box 708
Kent, OH 44240
(330) 678-1601
Fax: (330) 678-4526
Internet Address: www.ashaweb.org

Centers for Disease Control and Prevention
Bldg. 1 South, Room SSB249
1600 Clifton Rd. N.E.
Atlanta, GA 30333
(404) 639-3311
Internet Address: www.CDC.gov/

**Educational Resources Information
Center (ERIC)**
Clearinghouse on Teacher Information
One Dupont Circle N.W., Suite 610
Washington, DC 20036-1186
(202) 293-2450
Fax: (202) 457-8095
Internet Address: www.ericsp.org

National Health Information Clearinghouse
P.O. Box 1133
Washington, DC 20013-1133
(800) 336-4797
Internet Address: www.nhic-nt.health.org

Hearing

Better Hearing Institute
5021-B Blacklick Rd.
Annandale, VA 22003
(703) 642-0580
Internet Address: www.betterhearing.org

Heart Disease

American Heart Association
1150 Connecticut Ave. N.W., Suite 810
Washington, DC 20036
(202) 785-7900
Internet Address: www.americanheart.org

Kidney Disease

American Kidney Fund
6110 Executive Blvd., Suite 1010
Rockville, MD 20852
(301) 881-3052
Internet Address: www.arbon.com/kidney

National Kidney Foundation
30 East 33rd St., Suite 1100
New York, NY 10016
Internet Address: www.kidney.org

Mental Health

National Institute of Mental Health
Office of Scientific Information, Public
  Inquiries Section
5600 Fishers Lane, Room 7C-02
Rockville, MD 20892
(301) 443-4513
Internet Address: www. nimh.nih.gov

National Mental Health Association
1021 Prince St.
Alexandria, VA 22314
(703) 684-7722
Internet Address: www.nmha.org

Nutrition

Food and Drug Administration (FDA)
Office of Consumer Affairs
Public Inquiries
5600 Fishers Lane (HFE-88)
Rockville, MD 20857
(301) 827-4420

Physical Fitness

American Association for Health, Physical Education, Recreation, and Dance
1900 Association Dr.
Reston, VA 20191
(703) 476-3400
Fax: (703) 476-9527
Internet Address: www.aahperd.org

President's Council on Physical Fitness and Sports
200 Independence Ave. S.W., Suite 738-H
Washington, DC 20201
Internet Address:
   www.indiana.edu/ ~ preschal

Women's Sports Foundation
Eisenhower Parkway
East Meadow, NY 11554
(800) 227-3988
Internet Address:
   www.lifetimetv.com/wosport

Poisoning

See the emergency listings at the front of
the telephone directory for the Poison
Control Center number, or call directory
assistance for the toll-free hotline number
for your area.

Safety and First Aid

National Highway Traffic Safety Administration
U.S. Department of Transportation
400 7th St. S.W., Room 5130
Washington, DC 20590
(202) 366-0123
Internet Address: www.nhtsa.dot.gov

National Safety Council
1121 Spring Lake Dr.
Itasca, IL 60143-3201
(603) 285-1121
(800) 621-7615
Internet Address: www.nsc.org

Smoking

American Cancer Society
1599 Clifton Rd. N.E.
Atlanta, GA 30329
(404) 320-3333
(800) 227-2345
Internet Address: www.cancer.org

American Lung Association
1740 Broadway
New York, NY 10019
(212) 315-8700
Internet Address: www.lungUSA.org

Office of the Surgeon General
200 Independence Ave. S.W.
Room 716G
Washington, DC 20201
(202) 690-7694
Internet Address: www.dhhs.gov

Stress

American Institute of Stress
124 Park Ave.
Yonkers, NY 10703
(914) 963-1200
Internet Address: www.stress.org

Vision

American Council of the Blind
1155 15th St. N.W., Suite 720
Washington, DC 20005
(202) 467-5081
(800) 424-8666
Internet Address: www.acb.org

Harcourt Brace School Publishers

Dear Family Member,

In Chapter 1, Setting Goals, our class will be learning about self-respect—what it is and how it can help us make wise choices as we set and make plans to achieve goals. We will also learn some strategies for dealing with anger, stress, sadness, and grief. Finally, the chapter provides information about peer pressure and ways to resolve conflicts.

Family Activity

As a family, discuss the challenges that newcomers often face in becoming part of a community. Have family members share memories of times in their lives when they had to adjust to new surroundings. Have each person talk about the people who helped him or her adjust and how they helped.

Using the chart below, work together to list the names of recent newcomers to your neighborhood, school, or community. Have each family member suggest a way he or she could help make the newcomer welcome.

Welcome to the Community!

Name of Newcomer	Ways to Make the Newcomer Feel Welcome

Family Reading

The following books can help you and your family learn more about the topics covered in this chapter. Books should always be chosen with the approval of an adult family member.

- Beckelman, Laurie. *Body Blues*. Crestwood House, 1995. A discussion of body image and how it affects self-concept. EASY
- Van Draanen, Wendelin. *How I Survived Being a Girl*. HarperCollins, 1997. Twelve-year-old Carolyn, who has always wished she were a boy, begins to see things in a new light when her sister is born. AVERAGE
- Hyde, Margaret O. *Know About Mental Illness*. Walker & Co., 1996. Discusses many aspects of mental illness, including types, causes, cures, and misconceptions. ADVANCED

Thank you for participating in our study of health.

Sincerely,

Estimado familiar:

En el Capítulo 1, Establecer metas, nuestra clase aprenderá sobre el amor propio, qué es y cómo nos puede ayudar a hacer selecciones sabias a medida que establecemos y hacemos planes para alcanzar las metas. También aprenderemos algunas estrategias para tratar con el enojo, la estrés, la tristeza y la pena. Finalmente, el capítulo proporciona información sobre la presión de compañeros y maneras de resolver conflictos.

Actividad familiar:

En familia, comente los retos que enfrentan los recién llegados en una comunidad. Pida a los familiares que compartan los recuerdos de momentos en sus vidas cuando han tenido que adaptarse al ambiente que los rodea. Pida a cada persona que hable sobre la gente que lo ayudó a adaptarse y cómo lo ayudaron.

Usen la siguiente tabla para hacer una lista de los nombres de recién llegados a su vecindario, escuela o comunidad. Pida a cada familiar que sugiera una manera en que podría ayudar a darle la bienvenida al recién llegado.

¡Bienvenido a la comunidad!

Nombre del recién llegado	Maneras de hacer que el recién llegado se sienta bienvenido

Lectura familiar:

Los siguientes libros pueden ayudar a Ud. y a su familia a aprender más sobre los temas estudiados en este capítulo. Los libros siempre se deben elegir con la aprobación de un adulto de la familia.

- Beckelman, Laurie. *Body Blues.* Crestwood House, 1995. Una conversación sobre la imagen corporal y cómo afecta la dignidad. FÁCIL
- Van Draanen, Wendelin. *How I Survived Being a Girl.* HarperCollins, 1997. Carolyn de doce años de edad, que siempre ha deseado haber sido un niño, comienza a ver las cosas de otra manera cuando nace su hermana. INTERMEDIO
- Hyde, Margaret O. *Know About Mental Illness.* Walker & Co., 1996. Comenta muchos aspectos de las enfermedades mentales, incluidos tipos, causas, curas e ideas falsas. AVANZADO

Gracias por su participación en nuestro estudio de la salud.

Atentamente,

Harcourt Brace School Publishers

Dear Family Member,

In Chapter 2, Patterns of Growth, our class will be learning about the importance of being a responsible family member and the kinds of changes that affect families. We will also learn how heredity plays an important role in shaping the identity of each individual. Finally, we will discuss some of the physical and emotional changes that adolescence brings and learn strategies for coping with this stage in the life cycle.

Family Activity

Have your child use the following questions to interview a middle-aged or elderly adult family member about that person's experiences during his or her teenage years. Discuss the responses with your child. How have families changed? How have families remained the same?

Family Interview Sheet

1. Describe your family when you were a teenager.
2. What were your responsibilities?
3. How did your responsibilities change as you got older?
4. What was your favorite family activity?
5. Did you have a different favorite family activity as you got older?

Family Reading

The following books can help you and your family learn more about the topics covered in this chapter. Books should always be chosen with the approval of an adult family member.

- Tytla, Milan. *Come to Your Senses (All Eleven of Them)*. Annick Press Ltd., 1993. Students will love the activities in this fun and accessible book. Great illustrations and a strong glossary. EASY
- McDonald, Joyce. *Comfort Creek*. Delacorte Press, 1996. When her father loses his job, eleven-year-old Quinella and her family move from the security of a company mining town to an uncertain future in rural isolation. AVERAGE
- Schwartz, Linda. *What Do You Think? A Kid's Guide to Dealing with Daily Dilemmas*. Learning Works, 1993. This book helps young people address common situations and clarify their thinking regarding some of the dilemmas life presents. ADVANCED

Thank you for participating in our study of health.

Sincerely,

Estimado familiar:

En el Capítulo 2, Patrones de crecimiento, nuestra clase aprenderá sobre la importancia de ser un familiar responsable y los tipos de cambios que afectan a las familias. También aprenderemos cómo la herencia juega un papel importante en moldear la identidad de cada persona. Finalmente, comentaremos algunos cambios físicos y emocionales que llegan con la adolescencia y aprenderemos estrategias para tratar esta etapa en el ciclo de vida.

Actividad familiar:

Pida a su niño que use las siguientes preguntas para entrevistar a un familiar adulto sobre sus experiencias durante los años de su adolescencia. Comente con su niño las respuestas. ¿Cómo han cambiado las familias? ¿Cómo han permanecido iguales?

Hoja de entrevista familiar

1. Describe a tu familia siendo un adolescente.
2. ¿Cuáles fueron tus responsabilidades?
3. ¿Cómo cambiaron tus responsabilidades a medida que te hacías mayor?
4. ¿Cuál era tu actividad favorita?
5. ¿Tenías una actividad familiar favorita a medida que te hacías mayor?

Lectura familiar:

Los siguientes libros pueden ayudar a Ud. y a su familia a aprender más sobre los temas estudiados en este capítulo. Los libros siempre se deben elegir con la aprobación de un adulto de la familia.

- Tytla, Milan. *Come to Your Senses (All Eleven of Them)*. Annick Press, Ltd., 1993. Los estudiantes amarán las actividades en este libro divertido y accesible. Ilustraciones grandiosas y un glosario exigente. FÁCIL
- McDonald, Joyce. *Comfort Creek*. Delacorte Press, 1996. Cuando su papá pierde el trabajo, Quinella de once años de edad y su familia se mudan de la seguridad de un pueblo de una compañía minera a un futuro incierto en un aislamiento rural. INTERMEDIO
- Schwartz, Linda. *What Do You Think? A Kid's Guide to Dealing with Daily Dilemmas*. Learning Works, 1993. Este libro ayuda a los jóvenes a exponer situaciones comunes y clarificar sus pensamientos sobre los dilemas que presenta la vida. AVANZADO

Gracias por su participación en nuestro estudio de la salud.

Atentamente,

Name _____ Date _____

Dear Family Member,

In Chapter 3, Health and Fitness, our class will be learning about healthful habits for protecting skin, hair, nails, teeth, gums, vision, and hearing. The chapter stresses the importance of making wise choices when purchasing skin and hair products and provides strategies for helping students make these choices. We will also learn how to prevent computer-related health problems and how to exercise to maintain and promote physical fitness.

Family Activity

Many community organizations, such as hospitals, schools, YMCAs, and senior centers, offer low-cost physical fitness programs. Ask your child to find out about the programs available in your community. Help your child check a variety of advertising sources, such as local newspapers, supermarket bulletin boards, and phone books. Students can enter their findings on the following chart and share the chart with family members or neighborhood friends.

Fitness Programs in My Community

Description of Activity	Where	When	Phone Number

Family Reading

The following books can help you and your family learn more about the topics covered in this chapter. Books should always be chosen with the approval of an adult family member.

- Day, Trevor. *The Random House Book of 1001 Questions and Answers About The Human Body*. Random House, 1994. Invaluable reference book answers all questions. EASY
- Schwarzenegger, Arnold and Charles Gaines. *Arnold's Fitness for Kids Ages 11 to 14*. Doubleday, 1993. Outlines good health and nutrition as well as exercise programs. AVERAGE
- Hipp, Earl. *Fighting Invisible Tigers: A Stress Management Guide for Teens*. Free Spirit Publishing Inc., 1995. Guidance in managing stress. ADVANCED

Thank you for participating in our study of health.

Sincerely,

Estimado familiar:

En el Capítulo 3, La salud y mantenerse en forma, nuestra clase aprenderá hábitos saludables para proteger la piel, el cabello, las u–as, los dientes, las encías, la visión y la audición. El capítulo enfatiza la importancia de hacer selecciones sabias cuando compramos productos para la piel y el cabello y proporciona estrategias para ayudar a los estudiantes a hacer estas selecciones. También aprenderemos a cómo prevenir problemas de salud relacionados con la computadora y cómo ejercitar para mantener y promover la buena salud.

Actividad familiar:

Muchas organizaciones como los hospitales, las escuelas, el YMCA y los centros para los ancianos ofrecen programas de educación f'sica a bajo costo. Pida a su niño que descubra más sobre los programas disponibles de su comunidad. Ayude a su niño a que revise una variedad de recursos de promoción como periódicos locales, carteleras de supermercado y directorios telefónicos. Los estudiantes pueden entrar sus hallazgos en la siguiente tabla y compartir la tabla con familiares o amigos del vecindario.

Programas de educación física en mi comunidad

Descripción de la actividad	Dónde	Cuándo	Número telefónico

Lectura familiar:

Los siguientes libros pueden ayudar a Ud. y a su familia a aprender más sobre los temas estudiados en este capítulo. Los libros siempre se deben elegir con la aprobación de un adulto de la familia.

- Day, Trevor. *The Random House Book of 1001 Questions and Answers About the Human Body.* Random House, 1994. Libro de referencia inestimable responde todas las preguntas. FÁCIL

- Schwarzenegger, Arnold y Charles Gaines. *Arnold's Fitness for Kids Ages 11 to 14.* Doubleday, 1993. Líneas generales sobre buena salud y nutrición así como también programas de ejercicios. INTERMEDIO

- Hipp, Earl. *Fighting Invisible Tigers: A Stress Management Guide for Teens.* Free Spirit Publishing Inc., 1995. Guía para manejar el estrés. AVANZADO

Gracias por su participación en nuestro estudio de la salud.

Atentamente,

Harcourt Brace School Publishers

Name _____ Date _____

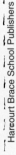

Dear Family Member,

In Chapter 4, Preparing Healthful Foods, our class will be learning the role that proteins, minerals, and vitamins play in a balanced diet. Material covered includes achieving a balanced diet with foods from around the world and the importance of not restricting food intake or overeating. In the final sections of the chapter, we will learn strategies for becoming a wise food consumer, including how to read food labels and how to ensure safe food preparation.

Family Activity

This chapter offers some opportunities for adding spice and variety to your family's weekly menu while ensuring that your family eats a well-balanced diet. With your child, prepare and serve one of the recipes presented in the chapter—Chicken Soft Tacos (page 153), Stir-Fried Broccoli and Carrots (page 155), or Fresh Spaghetti (page 157). Your child can then ask one or two family members to rate the dish.

Recipe: _____

Family Member	Comments

Family Reading

The following books can help you and your family learn more about the topics covered in this chapter. Books should always be chosen with the approval of an adult family member.

- Fitzsimmons, Cecilia. *All About Food Series: Vegetables & Herbs.* Silver Burdett Press, 1996. Well-designed, pithy information, colorful illustrations, recipes, and purposeful, fun activities. EASY
- Harbison, Elizabeth M. *Loaves of Fun.* Chicago Review Press, 1997. Lots of colorful illustrations and recipes make this a palatable way to learn about bread. AVERAGE
- Johnson, Sylvia A. *Tomatoes, Potatoes, Corn, and Beans: How the Foods of the Americas Changed Eating Habits Around the World.* Atheneum, 1997. Very informative, historical information for American eaters; black and white drawings. ADVANCED

Thank you for participating in our study of health.

Sincerely,

Estimado familiar:

En el Capítulo 4, Preparar alimentos saludables, nuestra clase aprenderá el papel que juegan las proteínas, los minerales y las vitaminas en una dieta balanceada. El material que se presenta incluye alcanzar una dieta balanceada con alimentos de todo el mundo y la importancia de no restringir la ingestión de alimentos o comer en exceso. En las secciones finales del capítulo, aprenderemos las estrategias para convertirse en un consumidor sabio incluidos cómo leer las etiquetas de los alimentos y la seguridad al preparar alimentos.

Actividad familiar:

Este capítulo ofrece algunas oportunidades para agregar sabor y variedad al menú semanal de su familia mientras asegura que su familia coma una dieta bien balanceada. Con su niño, prepare y sirva una de las recetas que se presentan en el capítulo—Tacos de pollo (página 153), brócoli y zanahorias fritas (página 155) o espaguetis (página 157). Luego, su niño puede preguntar a uno o dos familiares que evalúen el plato.

Receta: _____

Familiar	Comentarios

Lectura familiar:

Los siguientes libros pueden ayudar a Ud. y a su familia a aprender más sobre los temas estudiados en este capítulo. Los libros siempre se deben elegir con la aprobación de un adulto de la familia.

- Fitzsimmons, Cecilia. *All About Food Series: Vegetables & Herbs.* Silver Burdett Press, 1996. Buen diseño, información concisa, ilustraciones coloridas, recetas y actividades con propósito y divertidas. FÁCIL

- Harbison, Elizabeth M. *Loaves of Fun.* Chicago Review Press, 1997. Bastantes ilustraciones y recetas coloridas hacen de éste una manera apetitosa de aprender sobre pan. INTERMEDIO

- Johnson, Sylvia A. *Tomatoes, Potatoes, Corn, and Beans: How the Foods of the Americas Changed Eating Habits Around the World.* Atheneum, 1997. Información muy instructiva para los consumidores americanos; dibujos en blanco y negro. AVANZADO

Gracias por su participación en nuestro estudio de la salud.

Atentamente,

Harcourt Brace School Publishers

Name _____ Date _____

Dear Family Member,

In Chapter 5, Controlling Disease, our class will be learning some common risk factors that contribute to disease. Our class will also learn some of the symptoms and causes of infectious diseases, including sexually transmitted diseases and AIDS. The body's immune system often needs help fighting these diseases. Noninfectious diseases, such as heart disease and cancer, also pose health risks. Finally, our class will learn that the best way to stay healthy is to maintain a healthful lifestyle.

Family Activity

Organisms that cause infectious diseases are called pathogens. People frequently practice habits that spread pathogens. For example, people may share a glass of water or milk, or they may reuse silverware without washing it.

Ask your child to make a list in the space provided of habits that family members can practice to avoid the spread of infectious diseases. Discuss ways in which family members can help each other implement these practices.

Healthful Habits to Guard Against the Spread of Pathogens

Family Reading

The following books can help you and your family learn more about the topics covered in this chapter. Books should always be chosen with the approval of an adult family member.

- Collinson, Alan. *Facing the Future: Choosing Health.* Steck-Vaughn Publishers, 1991. Excellent resource for healthy decision-making and wellness; beautiful photography and easy-to-follow text. EASY
- Parker, Steve. *Medicine.* Dorling Kindersley, 1995. Fascinating historical information and visuals. AVERAGE
- Greenberg, Lorna. *AIDS: How It Works in the Body.* Franklin Watts, 1992. Examines how the AIDS virus invades the body and affects the immune system. ADVANCED

Thank you for participating in our study of health.

Sincerely,

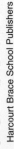

Nombre _____ Fecha _____

Estimado familiar:

En el Capítulo 5, Controlar enfermedades, nuestra clase aprenderá algunos factores de riesgo comunes que contribuyen con las enfermedades. Nuestra clase también aprenderá algunos de los síntomas y causas de enfermedades contagiosas incluidas las de transmisión sexual y el SIDA. El sistema inmunológico del cuerpo a menudo necesita ayuda para combatir estas enfermedades. Las enfermedades no contagiosas como las cardíacas y el cáncer también presentan riesgos a la salud. Finalmente, nuestra clase aprenderá que la mejor manera de estar saludable es mantener un estilo de vida saludable.

Actividad familiar:

Los organismos que causan enfermedades contagiosas se llaman patógenos. A menudo, la gente practica hábitos que propagan los patógenos. Por ejemplo, las personas pueden compartir un vaso de agua o leche o pueden usar de nuevo los platos sin lavarlos.

Pida a su niño que haga una lista de hábitos en el siguiente espacio que los familiares pueden practicar para evitar la propagación de enfermedades contagiosas. Comente las maneras en que los familiares pueden ayudarse para implementar estas prácticas.

Hábitos saludables para protegernos contra la propagación de enfermedades

Lectura familiar:

Los siguientes libros pueden ayudar a Ud. y a su familia a aprender más sobre los temas estudiados en este capítulo. Los libros siempre se deben elegir con la aprobación de un adulto de la familia.

- Collinson, Alan. *Facing the Future: Choosing Health.* Steck-Vaughn Publishers, 1991. Recurso excelente para tomar decisiones saludables inteligentes y bienestar; fotografías hermosas y texto fácil de leer. FÁCIL
- Parker, Steve. *Medicine.* Dorling Kindersley, 1995. Información y visuales históricas fascinantes. INTERMEDIO
- Greenberg, Lorna. *AIDS: How It Works in the Body.* Watts, 1992. Examina cómo el virus del SIDA invade el cuerpo y afecta el sistema inmunológico. AVANZADO

Gracias por su participación en nuestro estudio de la salud.

Atentamente,

Dear Family Member,

In Chapter 6, Drugs and Health, our class will be learning that, when used properly, prescription and over-the-counter medicines can help people recover from illnesses and stay healthy. However, when abused or misused, these medicines can have damaging effects. We will also learn about stimulants, depressants, marijuana, narcotics, and other illegal drugs. Strategies for saying *no,* for resisting peer pressure, and for recognizing the signs of drug abuse will also be addressed.

Family Activity

Prescription medicines are very strong drugs. Physicians order medicine for one person only. It is very important that only that person use the medicine and that the medicine be used only as directed.

Show your child a container of prescription drugs and point out the following information on the label: Name and address of the pharmacy, name of the doctor who prescribed the medicine, name of the patient, date on which the medicine was prescribed, name of the medicine, expiration date of the medicine, dosage, directions for use, warnings and cautions, and refill information. Explain what this information means, and reiterate that your child should take a medicine only with adult supervision.

Family Reading

The following books can help you and your family learn more about the topics covered in this chapter. Books should always be chosen with the approval of an adult family member.

- Gutman, Bill. *Harmful to Your Health.* Twenty-First Century Books, 1996. Straightforward presentation on the dangers of drug abuse. Special features, suggestions for change, and organizations to contact for help. EASY
- Gates, Phil. *The History News: Medicine.* Candlewick Press, 1997. History of medicine and healthcare presented in a newspaper-like format. AVERAGE
- Parker, Steve. *Medicine.* Dorling Kindersley Publishing, Inc., 1995. Provides history, techniques, and treatments from a global perspective. Wonderful color illustrations. ADVANCED

Thank you for participating in our study of health.

Sincerely,

Harcourt Brace School Publishers

Nombre _____ Fecha _____

Estimado familiar:

En el Capítulo 6, Las drogas y la salud, nuestra clase aprenderá que las medicinas con y sin receta cuando se usan adecuadamente pueden ayudar a la gente a recuperarse de enfermedades y mantenerse saludable. Sin embargo, cuando no se usan adecuadamente, estas medicinas pueden tener efectos perjudiciales. También aprenderemos sobre estimulantes, depresivos, marihuana, narcóticos y otras drogas ilegales. También se tratan las estrategias para decir *no*, para resistir la presión de compañeros y para reconocer las señales del mal uso de las drogas.

Actividad familiar:

Las medicinas con receta médica son drogas muy fuertes. Los médicos ordenan medicinas sólo para una persona. Es muy importante que sólo esa persona use la medicina y que sólo se use como se indica.

Muestre a su niño un recipiente de medicinas con receta médica y señale la siguiente información en la etiqueta: Nombre y dirección de la farmacia, nombre del médico que recetó la medicina, nombre del paciente, fecha en que se recetó la medicina, nombre de la medicina, fecha de vencimiento de la medicina, dosis, instrucciones de uso, advertencias y precauciones e información de segunda preparación. Explique lo que esta información significa y reitera que su niño sólo debe tomar una medicina bajo la supervisión de un adulto.

Lectura familiar:

Los siguientes libros pueden ayudar a Ud. y a su familia a aprender más sobre los temas estudiados en este capítulo. Los libros siempre se deben elegir con la aprobación de un adulto de la familia.

• Gutman, Bill. *Harmful to Your Health.* Twenty-First Century Books, 1996. Presentación directa de los peligros del abuso de drogas. Características especiales, sugerencias para cambiar y organizaciones para comunicarse en caso de ayuda. FÁCIL

• Gates, Phil. *The History News: Medicine.* Candlewick Press, 1997. La historia de la medicina y el cuidado de la salud se presentan en un formato como un periódico. INTERMEDIO

• Parker, Steve. *Medicine.* Dorling Kindersley Publishing, Inc., 1995. Provee la historia, las técnicas y los tratamientos desde una perspectiva global. Bellas ilustraciones a color. AVANZADO

Gracias por su participación en nuestro estudio de la salud.

Atentamente,

Name _____ Date _____

Dear Family Member,

In Chapter 7, Tobacco and Alcohol, our class will be learning the harmful short-term and long-term effects of using alcohol and tobacco. We will also learn how peer pressure and advertising contribute to alcohol and tobacco use. Finally, the chapter provides information about community agencies and recovery programs that can offer help if needed.

Family Activity

Ask your child to find out about local programs that provide young people with alternatives to drinking. Recreation centers, parks, and youth organizations frequently sponsor these programs. Ask your child to record his or her findings in the following chart. Then discuss the chart with your child. Work together to brainstorm other activities that could be made available.

Local Programs

Name of Program	Where	When	Phone Number

Family Reading

The following books can help you and your family learn more about the topics covered in this chapter. Books should always be chosen with the approval of an adult family member.

- Hyde, Margaret O. *Know About Smoking.* 3rd edition. Walker & Company, 1995. Discusses the dangers of tobacco use. EASY
- Monroe, Judy. *Alcohol.* Enslow Publishers, 1994. Information about alcohol and alcoholism, families, treatment, and prevention, with historical background of alcohol use. AVERAGE
- Pringle, Laurence. *Drinking—A Risky Business.* Morrow Junior Books, 1997. How alcohol was discovered, its effects, alcoholism, Prohibition, and alcohol advertising. ADVANCED

Thank you for participating in our study of health.

Sincerely,

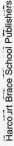

Estimado familiar:

En el Capítulo 7, El tabaco y las bebidas alcohólicas, nuestra clase aprenderá los efectos dañinos a corto y largo plazo de usar bebidas alcohólicas y tabaco. También aprenderemos cómo contribuyen al uso de bebidas alcohólicas y tabaco la presión de compañeros y la publicidad. Finalmente, el capítulo proporciona información sobre las agencias y los programas de recuperación de la comunidad que pueden dar ayuda.

Actividad familiar:

Pida a su niño que investigue sobre los grupos de apoyo locales que dan alternativas sobre la bebida a los jóvenes. Los centros de recreación, los parques y las organizaciones juveniles a menudo patrocinan estos programas. Pida a su niño que anote sus hallazgos en la siguiente tabla. Luego, comente la tabla con su niño. Juntos, piensen en otras actividades que podrían disponer.

Programas locales

Nombre del programa	Dónde	Cuándo	Número telefónico

Lectura familiar:

Los siguientes libros pueden ayudar a Ud. y a su familia a aprender más sobre los temas estudiados en este capítulo. Los libros siempre se deben elegir con la aprobación de un adulto de la familia.

- Hyde, Margaret O. *Know About Smoking.* Tercer edición. Walker and Company, 1995. Comenta los peligros del uso del tabaco. FÁCIL
- Monroe, Judy. *Alcohol.* Enslow Publishers, 1994. Información sobre las bebidas alcohólicas y el alcoholismo, las familias, el tratamiento y la prevención con antecedentes históricos del uso de bebidas alcohólicas. INTERMEDIO
- Pringle, Laurence. *Drinking—A Risky Business.* Morrow Junior Books, 1997. Cómo se descubrieron las bebidas alcohólicas, sus efectos, el alcoholismo, la prohibición y la publicidad de bebidas alcohólicas. AVANZADO

Gracias por su participación en nuestro estudio de la salud.

Atentamente,

Harcourt Brace School Publishers

Name _____ Date _____

Dear Family Member,

In Chapter 8, Safety and First Aid, our class will be learning about common safety hazards at home. We will also learn how to reduce the risk of injury while participating in water sports and during certain natural disasters, how first aid can be used to treat common injuries and save lives, and how to avoid situations that lead to violence.

Family Activity

It is important that your child be able to notify the proper authorities in case of an emergency. Have your child fill out the following emergency telephone list. Use your local telephone directory to obtain the correct phone numbers.

Have your child make one or more copies to place near home phones. Tell family members where the lists are located.

Emergency Telephone Numbers

Police	
Fire	
Poison control	
Ambulance	
Emergency	911 or 0 (zero)

Family Reading

The following books can help you and your family learn more about the topics covered in this chapter. Books should always be chosen with the approval of an adult family member.

- Gutman, Bill. *Recreation Can Be Risky*. Twentieth Century Books, 1996. Discusses safety in team sports, biking, swimming, street sports, and hiking. Presents weather dangers and first aid measures. EASY
- Goedecke, Christopher J. and Rosmarie Hausherr. *Smart Moves: A Kid's Guide to Self-Defense*. Simon & Schuster Books for Young Readers, 1995. Black and white photographs illustrate safety moves and offer alternatives to violence based on the martial arts. AVERAGE
- Kasdin, Karin. *Disaster Blaster: A Kid's Guide to Being Home Alone*. Avon Books, 1996. Offers practical advice on caring for younger siblings and for staying home alone. ADVANCED

Thank you for participating in our study of health.

Sincerely,

Estimado familiar:

En el Capítulo 8, Practicar la seguridad y los primeros auxilios, nuestra clase aprenderá sobre la seguridad con los peligros comunes en la casa. También aprenderemos cómo reducir el riesgo de accidentes mientras participamos en los deportes acuáticos y durante ciertos desastres naturales, cómo se pueden usar los primeros auxilios para tratar lesiones comunes y salvar vidas y cómo evitar situaciones que conducen a la violencia.

Actividad familiar:

Es importante que su niño sea capaz de notificar a las autoridades adecuadas en caso de una emergencia. Pida a su niño que llene la siguiente lista de teléfonos de emergencia. Use su directorio telefónico local para obtener los números telefónicos correctos.

Pida a su niño que haga una o más copias para colocarlas cerca de los teléfonos de la casa. Dígales a los familiares dónde están ubicadas las listas.

Números telefónicos de emergencia

Policía	
Bomberos	
Control de envenenamientos	
Ambulancia	
Emergencia	911 o 0 (cero)

Lectura familiar:

Los siguientes libros pueden ayudar a Ud. y a su familia a aprender más sobre los temas estudiados en este capítulo. Los libros siempre se deben elegir con la aprobación de un adulto de la familia.

- Gutman, Bill. *Recreation Can Be Risky*. Twentieth Century Books, 1996. Comenta la seguridad al practicar deportes en equipo, bicicleta, nado, deportes en la calle y escalar. Presenta los peligros del clima y las medidas de primeros auxilios. FÁCIL

- Goedecke, Christopher J. y Rosmarie Hausherr. *Smart Moves: A Kid's Guide to Self-Defense*. Simon and Schuster Books for Young Readers, 1995. Fotografías en blanco y negro ilustran movimientos seguros y ofrecen alternativas para la violencia basadas en las artes marciales. INTERMEDIO

- Kasdin, Karin. *Disaster Blaster: A Kid's Guide to Being Home Alone*. Avon Books, 1996. Ofrece consejos practicos sobre cuidar de hermanos menores y estar en casa solo. AVANZADO

Gracias por su participación en nuestro estudio de la salud.

Atentamente,

Harcourt Brace School Publishers

Dear Family Member,

In Chapter 9, Community Health, our class will be learning about community groups that prepare for natural disasters. We will also learn how family members can work together to prepare ahead of time for these disasters. Finally, the chapter provides information about community health services and the importance of using resources wisely and practicing conservation. Acid rain, toxic waste, and other environmental problems will also be discussed.

Family Activity

With your child, look through newspapers and newsmagazines to find articles about individuals and groups who have helped communities recover from natural disasters. Ask your child to choose his or her favorite article and summarize it in the space provided.

Discuss why your child chose this article and what the article tells him or her about the importance of people helping people in times of trouble.

People Helping People

Who	
What	
When	
Where	
Why	

Family Reading

The following books can help you and your family learn more about the topics covered in this chapter. Books should always be chosen with the approval of an adult family member.

- Milord, Susan. *Hands Around the World: 365 Ways to Build Cultural Awareness and Global Respect*. Williamson Publishing, 1992. Presents a variety of games and other activities to help children experience the daily lives of children from the far corners of Earth. EASY
- Pringle, Laurence. *Take Care of the Earth: Kids in Action*. Boyds Mill Press, 1996. How kids can care for the earth through environmental projects and actions. AVERAGE
- Hoff, Mary King. *Our Endangered Planet—Atmosphere*. Lerner Publications, 1995. Explains how the atmosphere works and how it is altered by pollutants. ADVANCED

Thank you for participating in our study of health.

Sincerely,

Estimado familiar:

En el Capítulo 9, La salud de la comunidad, nuestra clase aprenderá sobre los grupos que se preparan para los desastres naturales. También aprenderemos cómo los familiares se preparan de antemano para estos desastres. Finalmente, el capítulo provee información sobre los servicios de salud comunitarios y la importancia de usar los recursos sabiamente y practicar la conservación. También se comentan la lluvia ácida, los desperdicios tóxicos y otros problemas ambientales.

Actividad familiar:

Con su niño, busque en periódicos y revistas artículos sobre personas y grupos que han ayudado a las comunidades a recuperarse de los desastres naturales. Pida a su niño que elija su artículo favorito y lo resuma en el siguiente espacio.

Comente con su niño por qué eligió este artículo y lo que le dice el artículo sobre la importancia de gente que ayuda a la gente en momentos de dificultad.

Gente que ayuda a la gente

Quién	
Qué	
Cuándo	
Dónde	
Por qué	

Lectura familiar:

Los siguientes libros pueden ayudar a Ud. y a su familia a aprender más sobre los temas estudiados en este capítulo. Los libros siempre se deben elegir con la aprobación de un adulto de la familia.

- Milord, Susan. *Hands Around the World: 365 Ways to Build Cultural Awareness and Global Respect.* Williamson Publishing, 1992. Presenta una variedad de juegos y otras actividades para ayudar a los niños a experimentar las vidas diarias de niños de los extremos de la Tierra. FÁCIL
- Pringle, Laurence. *Take Care of the Earth: Kids in Action.* Boyds Mill Press, 1996. Cómo los niños pueden cuidar la Tierra mediante proyectos y acciones ambientales. INTERMEDIO
- Hoff, Mary King. *Our Endangered Planet—Atmosphere.* Lerner Publications, 1995. Explica cómo funciona la atmósfera y cómo la alteran los agentes contaminantes. AVANZADO

Gracias por su participación en nuestro estudio de la salud.

Atentamente,

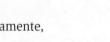

Harcourt Brace School Publishers

Activity Book Answer Key

The Amazing Human Body

Sense Organs

page 1

The sentences should be numbered as follows:

A. 3, 4, 7, 1, 6, 2, 5

B. 5, 1, 4, 3, 2

Skeletal System

page 2

1. Compact bone is the dense, outer bone tissue that surrounds spongy bone, a tissue with many spaces.
2. Blood vessels are located in the membrane that surrounds compact bone.
3. Red marrow is found in the center of the pelvis, the ribs, the vertebrae, the sternum, and the large bones of the arms and legs. Red marrow produces most blood cells.
4. Yellow marrow stores fats and is found in small bones such as those in the hands and the feet.

Muscular System

page 3

1. involuntary, cardiac
2. voluntary, striated
3. voluntary, striated
4. involuntary, smooth
5. involuntary, smooth
6. voluntary, striated
7. involuntary, smooth
8. voluntary, striated
9. voluntary, striated
10. voluntary, striated
11. voluntary, striated
12. voluntary, striated

Abdominal muscles are striated, voluntary muscles that contract to move your torso. Intestinal muscles are part of the intestines. When they contract, they move food along the digestive system. Intestinal muscles are involuntary smooth muscles.

Nervous System

page 4

1. brain and spinal cord
2. nerves
3. somatic and autonomic nervous systems
4. It takes messages from the central nervous system to the voluntary skeletal muscles.
5. It takes messages from the central nervous system to the involuntary smooth muscles in the organs in the body.
6. The body's autonomic nervous system produces these reactions.

The Lymphatic System

page 5

1. the fluid containing glucose, amino acids, other nutrients, oxygen, and a variety of salts that flows through the lymphatic system
2. Lymph nodes filter bacteria and other pathogens from lymph. The lymphatic system also produces a type of white blood cell that helps fight disease.
3. Glands swell when lymph nodes work hard to eliminate pathogens from lymph.
4. It returns fluid and nutrients to the bloodstream.

Chapter 1 • Setting Goals

Recognize Vocabulary *page 6*

1. i
2. a
3. d
4. j
5. f
6. e
7. h
8. b
9. c
10. g

Answers will vary. Possible answer: Melinda experiences stress whenever she takes a test. She feels anxiety about doing well. If she could improve her self-concept as a learner and test-taker, she would experience less stress.

Manage Stress *page 7*

Answers to questions 1–4 will vary. Possible answers are shown.

1. Being accidentally locked out of the house might cause the following physical reactions—butterflies in the stomach, nervous feeling, sweaty palms, upset stomach, and so on.
2. Being prepared can help a person stay calm. A child could talk to his or her parents and come up with ways to handle the situation, such as go to a trusted neighbor's home, return to school, call parent from pay phone.
3. Keeping calm goes a long way in handling the situation described here. The child should take a deep breath, think clearly, and remember the strategies already agreed to by the child and parent.
4. The child should put into action the best strategy from the approved list previously agreed to by the parent and child.

Draw Conclusions *page 8*

1. conflict
2. The disputants are the students who want to go to the DiMennas' and the students who want to go to the Fun Time Bowling Alley and Playland.
3. The class could turn to a mediator for help.
4. Answers will vary. Possible answer: The class might brainstorm other ideas for locations and activities for the class party. They also might brainstorm ways to play games at Mrs. DiMenna's house or ways to spend time at both locations.
5. The class might stop arguing and agree to disagree, listen to all sides of the conflict, negotiate, choose a solution, and write an agreement.

Resolve Conflicts *page 9*

Accept reasonable answers. Possible answers are shown.

1. Nadia: I think snakes are really interesting. Everyone will do boring animals like cats. Filomena: Snakes scare me. I love my cat, and I want to learn more about cats.
2. Nadia: I know snakes scare lots of people. But I want to study the ones in the Amazon. Filomena: I know lots of people will study cats. I am interested in the Amazon, too.
3. Nadia: If we are both interested in the Amazon, maybe we could study a different animal from there. Filomena: That's a good idea. Nadia: How about alligators? Filomena: They're pretty scary, too. Let's study an animal that is colorful.
4. Nadia: OK, I can agree to that. What about a macaw? Filomena: Yeah, macaws are really colorful birds that live in the Amazon. Let's do macaws.

Changing Stereotypes *page 10*

1. diversity
2. Possible answer: Stereotyping made Toshio's parents feel left out and hurt. It also hurt the people who closed their minds and hearts to their new neighbors.
3. Answers will vary. Possible answer: Yes. People made oversimplified judgments about their neighbors. They judged Toshio's parents as members of a group of outsiders instead of as individuals.
4. Possible answer: There is a great deal of diversity in Toshio's neighborhood. People there seem to have learned tolerance.

Use Context Clues *page 11*

1. collaborate
2. prejudice
3. peers
4. stereotypes
5. diversity
6. peer pressure
7. Conflicts
8. brainstorming
9. disputants
10. Conflict resolution
11. mediator
12. peer mediation

Chapter 2 • Patterns of Growth

Resolve Conflicts *page 12*
1. Accept reasonable answers. Answers should relate to the conflict resolution strategies. Possible answers: In any conflict, be willing to listen to the other person's point of view.
2. Ask for a mediator if you're having a problem.
3. Walk away, and leave time for a cooling-off period.
4. Use humor.

Use Pictorial Clues *page 13*
1. 2
2. 4
3. 1
4. 3

For the drawings of the stages of mitosis, refer to the illustrations on page 70 of the Pupil Edition.

Hereditary Traits *page 14*
1. brown or blue
2. Both parents have recessive genes for blue eyes, so Danelle's eyes could be blue. Both parents also have genes for brown eyes, so Danelle's eyes could be brown.
3. brown or blue
4. Evan has brown eyes but may have a recessive gene for blue eyes. Therefore, the children could have blue eyes. The mother has blue eyes, so she has no gene for brown eyes. However, Evan's gene for brown eyes could cause his children to have brown eyes.
5. They both may share many of the same inherited traits.

Use Vocabulary *page 15*
1. sperm
2. recessive
3. embryo
4. ovum
5. mitosis
6. chromosomes
7. responsible
8. sibling
9. nucleus
10. compromise
11. genes
12. heredity
13. fetus

Understanding Puberty and Growth
page 16
1. He is concerned that he will not grow enough to make the high school basketball team.
2. She has already begun her growth spurt. Lazelle has not.
3. Work on developing his basketball skills and continue to exercise, eat healthfully, and get adequate sleep.
4. Other students will begin their growth spurts soon and will likely get as tall as or taller than she is.

Reinforce Vocabulary
page 17
1. k
2. l
3. h
4. a
5. g
6. c
7. e
8. d
9. j
10. i
11. b
12. f

Possible answers: 1. When my body completes its final growth spurt, I will have reached my adult height. 2. By exercising every day, I am building stamina. 3. By following my family's rules and taking on responsibility, I am showing maturity.

Chapter 3 • Health and Fitness

Comparing and Contrasting *page 18*
Answers will vary. Possible answers are shown.
1. Both give information about D-Deodorant
2. The label lists the ingredients and directions. It also gives warnings and the name and address of the manufacturer. The advertisement highlights the name of the product, gives consumer information, and promises that the product will make the person popular.
3. Answers should include information on product ingredients, a comparison to other products' ingredients, and comparative pricing of other products.

Caring for Your Teeth *page 19*
I. B. Cavities can form.
II. A. Bad breath can develop.
   B. Calculus can form and lead to gum disease.
III. A. Avoid eating foods with a lot of sugar in them.
   B. Brush your teeth after eating.
   C. Use fluoride toothpaste when brushing.
   D. Use dental floss
   E. Eat a balanced diet high in calcium.
   F. Visit a dentist twice a year.

Use Word Meanings *page 20*
1. g	9. l
2. b	10. i
3. j	11. k
4. m	12. n
5. e	13. a
6. c	14. h
7. f	15. d
8. o	

Eye Problems and Solutions *page 21*

Eye Problems and Solutions	
Problem	Solution
Farsightedness	corrective lenses
Nearsightedness	corrective lenses
Astigmatism	corrective lenses
Conjunctivitis	a doctor's care
Sty	clean, warm compresses applied to the eye

Set Goals *page 22*
Possible answer: Fitness Goal: Improve cardiovascular fitness by running three days a week and improve muscle strength by doing curl-ups.

Day	Activity	How many	Number of Minutes
October 3	run		20 minutes
October 4	curl-ups	20	
October 5	run		20 minutes
October 6	curl-ups	20	
October 7	run		25 minutes
October 10	run		25 minutes
October 11	curl-ups	25	
October 12	run		27 minutes
October 13	curl-ups	25	

Analyze Vocabulary *page 23*
A. 1. a. muscular endurance
    b. muscular strength
    c. flexibility
    d. cardiovascular fitness
  2. a. conjunctivitis
    b. sty
    c. astigmatism
  3. a. repetitive strain injuries
    b. carpal tunnel syndrome
  4. Workout begining and end: warm-up, cool-down. Parts of a workout: aerobic exercise, anaerobic exercise.
B. Check to see that student sentences reflect an accurate understanding of fatigue, target heart rate, Activity Pyramid, workout, Calories, and decibels.

Chapter 4 • Preparing Healthful Foods

Identify the Main Idea and Important Details
page 24

1. You need water to digest food and transport nutrients to all the cells of your body.
2. You need water to take nutrients into your cells and build new cells.
3. Water helps keep your body temperature stable.
4. Water helps remove carbon dioxide, salts, and other wastes from your body.
5. You need water to keep your joints moving smoothly.

The Fats, Oils, and Sweets Group
page 25

1. Possible answers: French fries, doughnuts, fried chicken, candy, soda, butter, margarine, cookies, and jelly.
2. They might be included as a source of extra Calories for added energy.
3. A dentist might say that the sweets increase the likelihood of tooth decay. A physician might say that the fats could cause damage to the circulatory system, and the combination of fats and sugar could cause weight gain.

Recognize Vocabulary
page 26

1. sugar
2. cereal, pasta
3. substance that helps food move through the digestive system
4. cup of soup, slice of bread
5. calcium, iron
6. vegetable oil, butter
7. the nutrient your body needs most
8. type of sugar
9. nutrient that builds the body
10. the right amounts of five of the food groups
11. nutrients that help cause specific reactions in the body
12. person who doesn't eat meat
13. guide to good food choices
14. substance found in animal fats that can cause heart disease

Tips for Preparing Healthful Foods
page 27

1. stir-fry foods
2. steam foods
3. cook foods in a microwave oven
4. washing them first
5. eating them raw or cooking them only until tender
6. use seasonings instead of salt
7. substitute other sweeteners for sugar, such as fresh fruit

Make Decisions
page 28

Possible answers are shown. Accept reasonable answers.

Step 1 Ask what each food item is called and what it is made of. Think about the choices—eat everything; eat some items; eat nothing.

Step 2 I might feel sick; I might feel just fine; I might feel hungry.

Step 3 Eat at least some of the items, so I won't be hungry or offend the family.

Step 4 I experienced and enjoyed some new foods; my friend's family thought I was polite; they invited me to join them again for dinner at their home.

Use Word Meanings
page 29

1. nutritional deficiency
2. contamination
3. additives
4. anorexia
5. ingredients
6. convenience foods
7. recipe
8. preservatives
9. bulimia
10. staples

Chapter 5 • Controlling Disease

Some Environmental and Behavioral Risk Factors
page 30

1. Alcohol is a behavioral risk factor.
2. Alcohol and tobacco use by the same person greatly increases his or her chances of developing cancer.
3. Sunshine can be difficult to avoid, especially in low latitude regions. This makes it an environmental risk factor. Sunbathing and using tanning salons make UV radiation a behavioral risk factor.

Recognize Vocabulary
page 31

1. b
2. n
3. m
4. i
5. g
6. l
7. e
8. c
9. h
10. j
11. f
12. d
13. k
14. a

Compare and Contrast
page 32

1. Both prevent a person from developing a disease. Passive immunity occurs when the body passively acquires antibodies. Active immunity occurs when a person is exposed to antigens.
2. Antigens are foreign substances that stimulate the production of antibodies.
3. Natural passive immunity occurs when a woman passes antibodies to her child via breast milk or to an unborn child. Artificial passive immunity occurs when antibodies are injected into a person's body.

Recognize Vocabulary
page 33

1. f
2. m
3. a
4. c
5. i
6. h
7. k
8. d
9. g
10. j
11. n
12. b
13. l
14. e

Where There's Smoke, There's Fire!
page 34

1. Lung cancer is the second most common cancer in the United States.
2. Smoking is both an environmental (environmental tobacco smoke) and a behavioral risk factor.
3. Drinking alcohol as a smoker greatly increases a person's chances of developing lung and other types of cancer.
4. Environmental tobacco smoke contains more of some of the cancer-causing chemicals than smoke that is inhaled directly and can cause cancer in nonsmokers.

Manage Stress
page 35

1. Accept reasonable answers. Possible answers: too much homework, baseball team, piano lessons, peer pressure, difficult relationships with friends or family
2. Possible answers: tension from stress can cause sweating palms, upset stomach, dry mouth, irritability, and anger.
3. Possible answers: heart disease, strokes, automobile crashes, sports injuries, violent behavior.
4. Accept reasonable answers. Possible answers include: Heart disease: Exercise can release tension; time management can help you see exactly what can and can't be done in the time available, which helps make the problems reasonable and reduces the panic; eating a balanced diet can make sure your body has the nutrients it needs to deal with the stress.

Chapter 6 • Drugs and Health

Compare and Contrast
page 36

1. They both help people who are ill or injured; may ease pain or cure an illness; have labels that give important information; come in many different colors, shapes and forms; can have serious side effects. Misuse of either can be dangerous.
2. OTC medicines may be taken by anyone, but prescription medicines are to be used by only one particular person. Anyone can buy an OTC medicine, but a prescription medicine can only be bought by someone with a physician's order. OTC medicines are for minor illnesses and injuries that do not require the advice of a physician, but prescription medicines are usually for more serious physical problems.

Interpret Information
page 37

1. peer pressure
2. Yes, because she feels the need to take the same drug again and again.
3. Yes, because she needs more of the same drug to get the same effect.
4. addiction
5. withdrawal symptoms

Use Word Meanings
page 38

1. a
2. b
3. a
4. c
5. c
6. b
7. c
8. c
9. b
10. a
11. b
12. a

Analyze Vocabulary
page 39

	drug	stimulant	depressant	sometimes legal	always illegal	using it can harm you
amphetamines	+	+	–	+	–	+
cocaine	+	+	–	–	+	+
crack	+	+	–	–	+	+
cannabis	+	–	–	–	+	+
marijuana	+	–	–	–	+	+
hashish	+	–	–	–	+	+
narcotics	+	–	+	+	–	+
inhalants	+	?	?	+	–	+
hallucinogens	+	–	–	–	+	+

Apply Information
page 40

1. hallucinogens
2. stimulants, cannabis
3. narcotics, cannabis, depressants
4. lung congestion, violent behavior, hallucinations, as well as permanent brain, kidney, or liver damage
5. Yes, because heroin use can easily lead to addiction.

Refuse Illegal Drugs
page 41

Accept reasonable answers.

Chapter 7 • Tobacco and Alcohol

Nicotine: A Dangerous Drug
page 42

Possible answer: Tobacco is very harmful. It contains nicotine, which makes a person feel good for a while but is really bad in the long run. Cigarette smoke also contains carbon monoxide and tars that can hurt the heart, lungs, and air passages. Smokers can get serious diseases, which can lead to an early death.

Possible answer: Even though cigarettes are sold in the same stores that sell food, they contain a dangerous drug. Smokers have jobs and do school-work, but more people die as a result of smoking than from alcohol, car crashes, murders, suicide, illegal drugs, and fires combined.

Recognizing Vocabulary
page 43

1. b
2. f
3. g
4. e
5. d
6. a
7. c
8. Possible answers: Environmental tobacco smoke (ETS) harms everyone who breathes it, even people who don't smoke.
9. Nicotine in cigarettes is a poison that harms the body and can also make people addicted to cigarettes.

Alcohol: A Risky Business
page 44

1. It's dangerous for young people to use alcohol.
2. Alcohol affects a person's vision and balance.
3. Alcohol also affects judgment and a person's ability to make decisions.
4. People who have been drinking don't have the strength, stamina, or agility they would normally have.

5–6. Answers will vary. Accept answers that indicate that the student understands the risks associated with alcohol use.

Resisting Peer Pressure
page 45

1. Yes
2. No; Jarred could say he'd rather not have alcohol.
3. No; Louisa could say no, she feels like walking today.
4. Yes
5. No; Shanille should leave anyway.
6. Yes
7. Yes

Refusing Tobacco and Alcohol
page 46

Answers to questions 1–6 will vary. Possible answers are shown.

1. Say no and give a reason. "I can't spend the night at your house because I'm allergic to cigarette smoke."
2. Suggest something else to do. "Why don't you spend the night at my house?"
3. Use humor. "I'd sure like to, but my alligator can't stand the smoke."
4. You don't think the person offering alcohol will listen to your reasons, but you think saying no will be enough.
5. You don't think the person offering alcohol will listen to you and will keep pressuring you even after you say no.
6. A good friend offers you alcohol and you want to spend time together, but not drink alcohol.

Using Word Meanings
page 47

1. b
2. a
3. c
4. c
5. a
6. a
7. c
8. a

Accept paragraphs that indicate that the student understands and can use the words correctly.

Chapter 8 • Safety and First Aid

Use Word Meanings *page 48*
1. a tank filled with water or chemicals for putting out a fire
2. way to increase survival chances if caught in deep water
3. a strong rolling, shaking, or sliding of the ground
4. a storm with winds, snow, and cold temperatures
5. able to burn easily
6. a tall funnel of wind that whirls at very high speed
7. an unexpected situation that calls for quick action
8. a painful jolt caused by direct contact with electricity
9. a violent storm with high winds and heavy rain
10. a storm with strong winds, heavy rain, and lightning
11. an emergency situation

Be Prepared *page 49*
1. water in jugs, canned or packaged food, medicines, blankets, extra clothing, flashlights, battery-powered radio and batteries, nonelectric can opener
2. scissors and tweezers, hand cleaner, bandages, disposable latex gloves, plastic bags, cold packs, adhesive tape, gauze, antiseptic ointment, medicines needed by family members
3. **a.** Stay close to the ground, under the smoke.
   b. Yell "Fire!" to everyone in the home.
   c. Before opening your door, feel it with the back of your hand. If it is hot or warm, leave it closed. If it is cool, open it slowly and look around. Slam the door shut if you see heavy smoke or fire.
   d. Leave the building. Check all doors before you open them, and close any open doors.
   e. Meet your family at the place outside that you have agreed on.
   f. From a neighbor's home, call 911.
4. Summaries will vary but should include proper procedures to follow for each disaster.

Communicate *page 50*
Possible answers are shown. Accept reasonable answers.
1. Debbie knew she needed to call 911. She went to a pay phone.
2. Debbie told the dispatcher what had happened. She gave the location of the emergency and her name.
3. She answered the dispatcher's questions. She stayed on the line until the dispatcher told her she could hang up.
4. Debbie waited beside the young man until the emergency services responded.

Sequencing *page 51*
Sentences should be numbered as follows:
A. 4,5,3,1,2
B. 4,1,2,5,3

Recognizing Vocabulary *page 52*
1. d	7. a
2. e	8. g
3. c	9. j
4. i	10. h
5. b	11. k
6. l	12. f

Answers will vary. Accept all answers that show a correct understanding of the vocabulary terms.

Resolve Conflicts *page 53*
Possible answer: If they could stop and agree that they disagree, they could step back and put the whole thing in perspective. They could stop calling each other names, hurting each other, and allowing the situation to get out of hand. Then if they listened to each other, they might learn something useful about themselves, about the other person, or about their friendship. They can't negotiate about who will get the part, because the ultimate decision isn't up to them. It's up to whoever is casting the play, who in this case is a kind of mediator. But Beth and Katy could agree that each one has a right to do her best to try out for the part, and to accept the decision once it's made. They can compromise by agreeing to support whoever gets the part—whether it's one of them or someone else.

Chapter 9 • Community Health

Be Prepared! *page 54*

1. Juan Carlos's family has been shown how to use the fire extinguishers should an earthquake cause small, contained fires in and around the house. In the event of an earthquake or shortly thereafter, the wrench can be used to shut off the safety valve on the gas line.
2. Fires due to a broken gas line that leads to a hot water heater can be prevented if the hot water heater is secured to the basement wall.
3. In the event of an earthquake, emergency supplies should be readily accessible. Securing the trash can to the fence outside Benjamin's home likely will minimize damage or injury from the container should an earthquake occur.
4. Since they know first aid, the members of Kathy's family can help people who are hurt in an earthquake.

Recognizing Vocabulary *page 55*

1. shelter
2. Red
3. earthquake
4. flood
5. watch
6. tornado
7. blizzard
8. food
9. hurricane
10. Cross
11. warning
12. natural
13. disaster
14. thunder
15. storm
16. kit
17. lightning
18. evacuate

Identify Cause and Effect *page 56*

1. Cause: One car carrying four people uses less fuel than four cars carrying one person.
   Effect: riding in a carpool conserves energy
2. Cause: riding a bicycle doesn't use fossil fuel
   Effect: riding a bicycle is good for the environment
3. Cause: water the lawn in the evening or early in the morning
   Effect: the water won't evaporate in the heat of the day
4. Cause: all people in the United States keep their homes 6°F cooler
   Effect: save 570,000 barrels of oil every day
5. Cause: using insulation
   Effect: saves home heating energy
6. Cause: fixing broken windowpanes and leaky window frames
   Effect: stops air from leaking out

Some Types of Pollution *page 57*

Toxic wastes <u>leak</u> from drums.
Wastes then enter water, air, and <u>soil</u>.
Can cause <u>cancer</u>, <u>birth</u> <u>defects</u>, and other <u>health</u> <u>problems</u>

Motor vehicles produce <u>fumes</u>.
These fumes cut off oxygen to the <u>heart</u>, which can trigger <u>heart</u> <u>attacks</u>.

Burning coal produces <u>chemicals</u>
that can be inhaled.
This can damage <u>lungs</u>.

that come into contact with skin.
This can cause <u>skin</u> <u>cancer</u>.

Using Context Clues *page 58*

1. l
2. d
3. j
4. c
5. a
6. g
7. m
8. i
9. k
10. h
11. b
12. e
13. f

Set Goals *page 59*

Possible answers are shown. Accept reasonable answers.

1. Earn $5.00 by recycling soft drink cans and bottles.
2. Call recycling centers and choose the center that offers the best value. Determine how many cans and bottles I need to collect during the month to earn $5.00. Collect cans and bottles at home and in the neighborhood. Turn in the cans and bottles I collect.
3. Each week, count the number of cans and bottels I collect to see whether I am reaching my goal. Keep track on a calendar.
4. See how much money I have earned at the end of the month. Decide whether I want to continue the project or change it.